P9-CQZ-162

THE
INTEGRITY
CRISIS

Warren W. Wiersbe

THE INTEGRITY CRISIS

A Division of Thomas Nelson Publishers
Nashville

Copyright © 1988 by Warren W. Wiersbe

All rights reserved. Written permission must be secured from the publisher to use or reproduce any part of this book, except for brief quotations in critical reviews or articles.

Published in Nashville, Tennessee, by Oliver-Nelson Books, a division of Thomas Nelson, Inc., Publishers, and distributed in Canada by Lawson Falle, Ltd., Cambridge, Ontario.

Unless otherwise noted, Scripture quotations are from THE NEW KING JAMES VERSION. Copyright © 1979, 1980, 1982, Thomas Nelson, Inc., Publishers.

The Scripture quotation noted J. B. Phillips is from J. B. Phillips: THE NEW TESTAMENT IN MODERN ENGLISH, Revised Edition. © J. B. Phillips 1958, 1960, 1972. Used by permission of Macmillan Publishing Co., Inc.

The Scripture quotation noted the New International Version of the Bible is taken from the HOLY BIBLE: NEW INTERNATIONAL VERSION. Copyright © 1973, 1978, 1984 by the International Bible Society. Used by permission of Zondervan Bible Publishers.

Printed in the United States of America.

Library of Congress Cataloging-in-Publication Data

Wiersbe, Warren W.
  The integrity crisis.

  Bibliography: P.
  1. Christianity—20th century. 2. Christian
life—1960–   . I. Title.
BR121.2.W46 1988   262'.7   88–1771
ISBN 0-8407-9091-0

1 2 3 4 5 6 — 92 91 90 89 88

Dedicated to the memory of

THEODORE H. EPP
(1907–1985)

Founder and Bible teacher of
"Back to the Bible" broadcast
A man of the Word
A man of integrity

We have become a reproach to our
*   neighbors,*
A scorn and derision to those who are
*   around us.*

Oh, do not remember former iniquities
*   against us!*
Let Your tender mercies come speedily
*   to meet us. . . .*

Help us, O God of our salvation,
For the glory of Your name;
And deliver us, and provide atonement
*   for our sins.*

PSALM 79:4, 8–9

CONTENTS

PREFACE

This has been a difficult book to write, because in it I've
had to be critical of some things that are very close to my
heart. That always hurts.

I've pastored three churches, and it pains me to have to
point out where we in the church have failed. If some unbe-
liever reads this book looking for ammunition, let me make it
clear that I'd rather be a struggling Christian in an imperfect
church than a perfect sinner outside the church. One of the
church fathers said that the church was something like Noah's
ark: if it weren't for the judgment on the outside, you could
never stand the smell on the inside.

As an author, an editor, and a radio preacher, I have in-
vested a lot of time, money, and energy into ministering
through the media, and I'm sympathetic to the problems of

publishers and producers. But this doesn't blind me to the fact that media ministries are in trouble and we must face things honestly. I hope none of my friends in radio, TV, and publishing think I'm picking on them. Believe me, the pronoun I'm using is *we* and not *they*. I want to write as a witness and not as a prosecuting attorney. We are all in this together.

No doubt this will be a troublesome book for some people to read. I have tried to write carefully and compassionately; but human nature being what it is, somebody is bound to misunderstand something I have said. You will miss the point if you look in these pages for this organization or that preacher. *This book is about all of us and the crisis we are in.* It's not an autopsy on somebody else's corpse. It involves all of us who profess to trust and serve Jesus Christ.

Well, if I'm misunderstood, I'm misunderstood. The Lord knows my heart, and He's the final Judge. "Is it so bad, then, to be misunderstood?" asked Emerson. "Pythagoras was misunderstood, and Socrates, and Jesus, and Luther, and Copernicus, and Galileo, and Newton."[1] While I'm certainly not in their ball park, it's comforting to know that I'll have such good company.

I thank God that I've had the privilege of living during this exciting era in the history of His church. The only other time I would have chosen is the Victorian era in Britain, but nobody gave me the opportunity to vote. I thank God that He has permitted me to have a very small part in His work during these years and to be associated with some of the giants of this day. They have been very kind to me and I should show my gratitude by listing their names here, but I won't. If I did, some of them would be surprised to discover they were giants!

There are things in this book I have wanted to say for a long time, and I would have said them even had there been no media scandal. Pearlygate is not the theme of this book; it's just the event that helped to pull my thoughts together. At the morning worship service of the 1987 Christian Booksellers Convention, I gave a message from Nehemiah, "Rebuilding in a Day of Reproach"; and my good friend Dr. Victor Oliver urged me to expand it into a book. Victor is difficult to refuse, so I gave in. Had I known how painful this experience would be, I probably would have argued with him a little longer.

These are serious days for the church, and the time is short. I know, preachers have been saying that ever since Paul's day, but it's still true. God has given us an unprecedented opportunity to reach our world with the gospel, but we can't do it right without personal and organizational integrity.

I'm not anxious that you agree with everything I've written. I'm anxious that you bow with me and say, "Lord, is it I?"

That's where real integrity begins.

WARREN W. WIERSBE

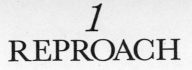

1
REPROACH

Scandal: vice enjoyed vicariously.

ELBERT HUBBARD

If I were to ask you to describe in one word the present situation of the church as you see it, what word would you select?

Revival? I doubt it, but I wish it were true! We see a good deal of evangelism going on today, and we're thankful for it; but the wind of the Spirit seems very still, and the atmosphere is rather stuffy.

Renewal? Perhaps in some ministries; but for the most part, it's "business as usual." It will take more to move the church than rearranging the worship service and hanging up a few banners.

Reassessment? Yes, a lot of studies are going on, and we hope they will be useful. But I fear that the church body is getting an autopsy at a time when it really needs a resurrection.

Ruin? Not as long as God is on the throne and there are people willing to listen and obey! No matter how dark the hour, the stars are still shining; but we'll have to look up to see them. I'm a realist, but I'm not a pessimist.

After a good deal of thought, I've come to the conclusion that the one word that best describes the evangelical church situation today is *reproach,* and I have a feeling that many people agree with me. In fact, *reproach* is the one word that seems to describe other areas of society besides the church: the sports arena, the embassy, the halls of academe, the White House, the Pentagon, Wall Street, Capitol Hill, and even the day-care center. Scandal seems to be the order of our day. We've had Watergate, Koreagate, and Irangate; and now the latest scandal is Pearlygate. No wonder *Time* asked in its cover story for May 25, 1987, "What Ever Happened To Ethics?"

What ever *did* happen to ethics? Perhaps nothing has happened. Perhaps society is still fairly ethical, and these nasty situations are not really scandals at all but only the results of good reporting and wider news coverage. After all, there have always been scandals—in government, in big business, in sports, and even in the church—so why get excited? The church has had its share of hypocrites and religious hucksters almost from the beginning, and the tares and wheat will grow together until the Lord returns. Then why get all worked up? This too shall pass.

The explanation is not quite that simple. If it were, all we'd have to do is bide our time until some new scandal hit the headlines and the public lost interest in the church's dirty linen. But the problem is not that simple, nor is the solution that easy. Why? Because the crisis the church is facing today cuts to the very heart of its authority and its ministry.

Our problem is not that the public has suddenly found sinners in the church, much to the embarrassment of Christians. No, the public has known about sin in the church for a long time; and somehow the church has survived. Evangelical Christians today are not like a group of schoolchildren, standing around blushing because we were caught breaking the rules. We are more like a defeated army, naked before our enemies, and unable to fight back because they have made a frightening discovery: the church is lacking in integrity.

If this discovery were only that the church is infected with hypocrites, all we would have to do is take off our masks, apologize, and start being honest again. But the matter goes much deeper than most of us want to admit, because integrity involves the very *nature* of the church in the world today. The diagnosis is painful and the remedy costly, but the church must have the courage to face them honestly and do what needs to be done.

We are facing an *integrity* crisis. Not only is the *conduct* of the church in question, but so is the very *character* of the church. The world is asking, "Can the church be trusted?" and *how* we answer is as important as *what* we answer.

For nineteen centuries, the church has been telling the world to admit its sins, repent, and believe the gospel. Today, in the twilight of the twentieth century, the world is telling the church to face up to her sins, repent, *and start being the true church of that gospel.* We Christians boast that we are not ashamed of the gospel of Christ, but perhaps the gospel of Christ is ashamed of us. For some reason, our ministry doesn't match our message. Something is wrong with the church's integrity.

The church has grown accustomed to hearing people question the *message* of the gospel, because that message is foolishness to the lost. But today the situation is embarrassingly reversed, for now the *messenger* is suspect. Both the ministry and the message of the church have lost credibility before a watching world, and the world seems to be enjoying the spectacle. "Why should we listen to the church?" the critical world is asking. "By what authority do you Christians preach to us about sin and salvation? Set your own house in order and then we may want to listen to you."

Of course, we have our ammunition ready. "Why don't you people set *your* house in order?" we ask. "The football scandals haven't kept you out of the stadium or made you turn off your television sets on weekends. The Wall Street scandals didn't disgust you so much that you took your money out of the bank or cashed in your investments. Will you stop voting because over a hundred administration officials have been accused of questionable activities and some of them have had to resign? No! Then why reject the church because a few people may not have practiced what they preached?" So there!

This defense sounds logical, except that it's based on two dangerous misunderstandings of the real nature of the crisis that the church is facing today.

To begin with, the integrity crisis involves more than a few people who were accused of moral and financial improprieties. *The integrity crisis involves the whole church.* I am not saying that people didn't sin, nor am I preaching "collective guilt," whatever that is. I only want to emphasize that, in the body of Christ, we belong to one another, we affect one another, and we can't escape one another. The press did not create the crisis, the church did; and the church will have to solve it. "And if one member suffers, all the members suffer with it," wrote Paul, "or if one member is honored, all the members rejoice with it" (1 Cor. 12:26). Whether we like it or not, we are all in this thing together.

It is the thesis of this book that Pearlygate is the symptom of critical problems in the evangelical world, problems so deep and serious that they won't be solved by quick fixes. Preaching about integrity, appointing new leaders, and setting up tougher standards of fiscal accountability may help, but they will touch only the surface. The church does not need a cosmetician; it needs a surgeon.

There is a second reason why this defense is faulty: *the weakness of the church helped to cause these scandals.* The church is the salt of the earth, but apparently we are not salty enough to hinder corruption in government, big business, sports, or even religious ministry. The church is the light of the world, but that light is apparently too weak to have much of an influence on today's movers and shakers.

And how strange that these scandals occurred at a time when many Christians were boasting of the strength and popularity of conservative Christianity! After all, we have crowded churches, radio and TV ministries, large conventions, respected Christian writers and musicians, Christian bookstores, Bible classes and chapels in colleges, universities, government and business offices, and even locker rooms. Some of our key church leaders are interviewed over network radio and TV programs, and some leaders are influencing the political scene. But in spite of these and other achievements, the scandals came just the same. Something is bound to be wrong.

I'm not criticizing the people and organizations promoting these ministries; in fact, I'm involved in some of them, and I thank God for the witness of His people in all these places. But I must point out that something is radically wrong when evangelical ministry can be so popular and yet at the same time be so weak. Perhaps its popularity is its weakness; after all, reputation and character are two different things. Apparently our right hand doesn't know what our left hand is doing, and as a result, our message and our ministry are divided.

It's a matter of integrity, so let's start there.

2
REGRESSION

God made integers, all else is the work of man.

LEOPOLD KRONECKER

In order to understand integrity, we must first realize that two forces are at work in our world today: (1) God is putting things together, and (2) sin is tearing things apart. God wants to make integers; Satan wants to make fractions. God's purpose is to "gather together in one all things in Christ" (Eph. 1:10), and He cannot accept neutrality. "He who is not with Me is against Me, and he who does not gather with Me scatters" (Luke 11:23). God's program will finally succeed, and His universe will one day become one glorious integer. But until that happens, you and I must live in a fractional world and experience the problems that come from fragmentation.

The church is God's chief instrument in this world for putting things together; and in order to do the job right, the church itself must have wholeness. If there is one place where the shattered people of our fractured society ought to find integrity, it is in the local church. After all, we Christians are reconciled to God and united to one another, so people have every right to expect to see integrity in the church.

What is *integrity?* The *Oxford English Dictionary* says that the word comes from the Latin *integritas,* which means "wholeness," "entireness," "completeness." The root word is *integer,* which means "untouched," "intact," "entire." Integrity is to personal or corporate character what health is to the body or 20/20 vision is to the eyes. A person with integrity is not divided (that's *duplicity*) or merely pretending (that's *hypocrisy*). He or she is "whole"; life is "put together," and things are working together harmoniously. People with integrity have nothing to hide and nothing to fear. Their lives are open books. They are integers.

Here is how Jesus described integrity:

> Do not lay up for yourselves treasures on earth, where moth and rust destroy and where thieves break in and steal; but lay up for yourselves treasures in heaven, where neither moth nor rust destroys and where thieves do not break in and steal. For where your treasure is, there your heart will be also.
>
> The lamp of the body is the eye. If therefore your eye is good, your whole body will be full of light. But if your eye is bad, your whole body will be full of darkness. If therefore the light that is in you is darkness, how great is that darkness!
>
> No one can serve two masters; for either he will hate the one and love the other, or else he will be loyal to the one and despise the other. You cannot serve God and mammon (Matt. 6:19–24).

Jesus made it clear that integrity involves the whole of the inner person: the heart, the mind, and the will. The person with integrity has a *single heart*. He doesn't try to love God and the world at the same time. His heart is in heaven, and that's where his treasure is. "Do not love the world or the things in the world. If anyone loves the world, the love of the Father is not in him" (1 John 2:15). An integrated person takes this command seriously: "You shall love the LORD your God with all your heart" (Matt. 22:37).

The person with integrity also has a *single mind,* a single outlook ("eye") that keeps life going in the right direction. After all, outlook helps to determine outcome; "a double-minded man [is] unstable in all his ways" (James 1:8). Lot was a double-minded man, which helps to explain why he chose a house in Sodom instead of a tent in the holy camp of Abraham (see Gen. 13:6ff.). The thing that helped to keep Abraham on the right track was his single vision. He was a stranger and pilgrim on earth with his eyes of faith firmly fixed on God and the heavenly city (see Heb. 11:13–16).

Jesus also said that the person with integrity has a *single will;* he seeks to serve but one master. Peter T. Forsythe was right when he said, "The first duty of every soul is to find not its freedom but its Master."[1] Once you find your Master, Jesus Christ, you will find your freedom; "therefore if the Son makes you free, you shall be free indeed" (John 8:36). Nobody can successfully serve two masters. To attempt to do so is to become a fractional person, and a fractional person doesn't have integrity. He is someone with a divided heart, a divided mind, and a divided will.

Of all the well-known servants of God I've been privileged to work with, none exemplified integrity more than Theodore H. Epp, founder of Back to the Bible. Repeatedly he reminded the staff and the board that God didn't call him and the organization to try to do everything. "This one thing I do!" was his controlling principle. He graciously turned down some of my "best suggestions" because he saw that they would get us on detours. Not only was he afraid of detours, but he was also afraid of becoming a "popular preacher" that pleased everybody.

During one period of his ministry, he came to the conclusion that something was wrong because he wasn't receiving any critical mail. (Most media preachers would welcome that!) He went on a brief spiritual retreat, searched his heart, and came back with plans for a series of messages that would challenge his listeners. He wasn't trying to be a crusader, deliberately looking for trouble; he just didn't want to be a coward, trying to avoid trouble.

He said, "I'm afraid that when I'm pleasing everybody, I'm not pleasing the Lord; and pleasing the Lord is what counts."

Jesus explained that the "single eye" lets in the light while the "double eye"—two outlooks on life and two masters in life—creates darkness within. Then He warned that *the person without integrity actually thinks that the darkness is light!* This frightening process of moral and spiritual deterioration is described by the apostle John:

> This is the message which we have heard from Him and declare to you, that God is light and in Him is no darkness at all. If we say that we have fellowship with Him, and walk in darkness, we lie and do not practice the truth (1 John 1:5–6).

This is step one toward inner darkness—hypocrisy, *lying to other people* about our fellowship with the Lord. There are many ways we can do this: preaching what we don't practice, praying things we don't mean, pretending to do what we don't do. But pretense is only the beginning, for the problem gets worse. John went on to say:

If we say that we have no sin, we deceive ourselves, and
the truth is not in us (1 John 1:8).

The situation indeed is growing more serious, for now we are
not only lying to others, but we are also *lying to ourselves and believing it!* Hypocrisy has now become duplicity. We are no
longer only pretending; lying has now become a way of life for
us, and we see nothing wrong with it. Hypocrisy has given
way to duplicity.

Where does it end?

If we say that we have not sinned, we make Him a liar,
and His word is not in us (1 John 1:10).

Now we are not only lying to others and to ourselves, but *we are
trying to lie to God and, in so doing, making God a liar!* We can even
read God's Word and feel no conviction of sin. Why? Because
the moral decay within has turned the light into darkness. Hypocrisy has become duplicity, and duplicity has produced
apostasy. And it all started with a double heart that encouraged a double mind and a divided will.

The only way to avoid this tragedy is to "walk in the light"
and keep the inner person honest and clean before God
(1 John 1:7, 9). We must become "one thing" people: "one
thing I do" (Phil. 3:13); "one thing I have desired" (Ps.
27:4); "one thing is needed" (Luke 10:42). We must follow
Paul's counsel: "If then you were raised with Christ, seek
those things which are above, where Christ is, sitting at the
right hand of God. Set your mind on things above, not on
things on the earth" (Col. 3:1-2).

What John has to say about the individual believer also applies to churches and ministries collectively, for ministries are

made up of individual believers, all of whom are members of the body of Christ. We belong to one another, we need one another, we affect one another, and we can't escape one another.

Therefore, when *hypocrisy* (lying to others) and *duplicity* (lying to oneself) start to take over, integrity gradually erodes until it is finally destroyed. The result is always *apostasy* (making God a liar), and gradually the light becomes darkness. And all this takes place *while the person or the ministry is maintaining what appears to be a faithful relationship with God.* When the crash comes, people are surprised and shocked. In fact, the sinners themselves are surprised and will even defend themselves against their accusers. The light has become darkness, and they can no longer discern right from wrong.

Integrity means that the light is shining within because the person (or group) has a single heart, a single mind, and a single will. Hypocrisy means that fractions have formed and the shadows have moved in. Duplicity means that the light has become darkness, wrong has become right, and sin has become acceptable. That is the kind of person Jesus had in mind when He said:

> Not everyone who says to Me, "Lord, Lord," shall enter the kingdom of heaven, but he who does the will of My Father in heaven. Many will say to Me in that day, "Lord, Lord, have we not prophesied in Your name, cast out demons in Your name, and done many wonders in Your name?" And then I will declare to them, "I never knew you; depart from Me, you who practice lawlessness!" (Matt. 7:21–23).

Saying the right words, carrying the right credentials, giving sermons from the right texts, helping people with their problems, and even performing miracles can never take the place of doing the will of God. The tragedy today, however, is that many people can't tell the difference between the real and the counterfeit; and what the majority calls "blessing" may actually be a judgment from God!

Perhaps the best illustration of this tragedy is the nation of Israel, so let's go back in history and meet two men of courage and integrity: Nehemiah and Jeremiah. They can teach us a great deal about what is happening in the church today and what you and I should be doing about it.

3
REBELLION

---

*The ultimate proof of the sinner
is that he does not know
his own sin.*

MARTIN LUTHER

The crisis the church is facing today is similar to the one Jeremiah and his people faced in the days just before the Babylonian captivity. It's also similar to the one Nehemiah faced when he risked his life to rebuild what the enemy had destroyed. Jeremiah spent forty years trying to prevent the crisis, and Nehemiah came along a century later and tried to remove the shame that the crisis had left behind. Both men lived in days of reproach.

"We lie down in our shame," wrote Jeremiah. "And our reproach covers us" (3:25). God said to the nation through His prophet, "And I will bring an everlasting reproach upon you, and a perpetual shame, which shall not be forgotten" (23:40). After Jeremiah witnessed the city and the temple being destroyed, he prayed, "Remember, O LORD, what has come upon us; / Look, and behold our reproach!" (Lam. 5:1).

The situation was the same when Nehemiah arrived on the scene. "The survivors who are left from the captivity in the province are there in great distress and reproach. The wall of Jerusalem is also broken down, and its gates are burned with fire" (Neh. 1:3). Jerusalem was no longer "Beautiful in elevation, / The joy of the whole earth, / . . . The city of the great King" (Ps. 48:2).

Here's what Nehemiah reported after he had investigated things for himself: "You see the distress that we are in, how Jerusalem lies waste, and its gates are burned with fire. Come and let us build the wall of Jerusalem, that we may no longer be a reproach" (Neh. 2:17).

Asaph the psalmist wrote,

> O God, the nations have come into
>   Your inheritance;
> Your holy temple they have defiled;
> They have laid Jerusalem in heaps. . . .
> We have become a reproach to our neighbors,
> A scorn and derision to those who are
>   around us (Ps. 79:1, 4).

What happened that the city of rejoicing became a city of reproach? We must answer that question honestly because the church is in a similar danger today *and God's judgment is threatening*. To find the answer, we must listen to the prophet Jeremiah. He saw the destruction of Jerusalem coming, he lived through it, and he can explain better than anyone else just why and how it happened. Then we'll return to Nehemiah and learn how God wants us to rebuild in a day of reproach.

In the eighteenth year of Josiah, the last good king of Judah, Hilkiah the high priest found a copy of the Book of the Law (probably Deuteronomy) while the temple was being repaired. Shaphan read the book to the king; and when Josiah heard the Word of God, he humbled himself and called the nation to repentance. He led the people in removing idolatry from the land and restoring the worship of Jehovah, at least outwardly. This event is recorded in 2 Kings 22–23 and is usually called "the great revival under Josiah." The reformation accomplished some good things, but I doubt that what happened could honestly be called a "revival." At least, Jeremiah didn't think so.

Jeremiah had been prophesying about five years when Josiah's religious reformation began, and he initially cooperated with it. But then he began to see that essentially *nothing was changing in the spiritual life of the nation.* By executive fiat, Josiah could remove the idols from the land, but he could not remove the idols from the hearts of the people. Yes, there was a remnant of sincere worshipers in the land, but for the most part, the revival was both shallow and temporary. The old-time religion was fashionable, and everybody wanted to be in step with the times.

We know that the revival was only a temporary popular movement because of what happened after King Josiah died and his son Jehoahaz took over. The new king led the people right back into their former sins, *and they followed him gladly.* Think of it: Josiah's own son had not even bowed the knee to Jehovah! "As soon as the influence of the court was withdrawn," wrote Joseph Parker, "it was seen that the people had not undergone the process of spiritual conviction."[1]

Now we can better understand why Jeremiah was mistreated for so many years and why his message was rejected: he saw through the false religion of his day and dared to tell the truth about it, even though doing so meant loneliness, persecution, and martyrdom. To the prophets and priests, he was a heretic; to the politicians and common people, he was a traitor. The majority of the people in Judah joined the religious parade, but Jeremiah marched to a different drummer.

It's likely that Jeremiah was silent during the reformation years of Josiah; but when Jehoahaz was crowned, the prophet broke his silence. He preached a courageous sermon while standing at one of the gates of the temple. It's recorded in Jeremiah 7:1–8:3, and I urge you to read it. Imagine how members of the average evangelical congregation today would respond if they heard this kind of preaching next Sunday morning.

> Amend your ways and your doings, and I will cause you to dwell in this place. Do not trust in these lying words, saying, "The temple of the LORD, the temple of the LORD, the temple of the LORD are these."
>
> Behold, you trust in lying words that cannot profit, Will you steal, murder, commit adultery, swear falsely, burn incense to Baal, and walk after other gods whom you do not know, and then come and stand before Me in this house which is called by My name, and say, "We are delivered to do all these abominations"? Has this house, which is called by My name, become a den of thieves in your eyes? (Jer. 7:3–4, 8–11).

The well-known Bible expositor G. Campbell Morgan reminds us that a "den of thieves" is the place where thieves run to hide after they have committed their crimes. One of the best ways to cover our sins is to attend a religious service and go through the motions of worshiping God, carefully avoiding any feelings of repentance. "These people draw near to Me with their mouth, / And honor Me with their lips, / But their heart is far from Me" (Matt. 15:8, quoting Isa. 29:13).

The orthodox religion of Jeremiah's day was incredibly like what passes for orthodox Christianity in our own day. For one thing, what the people professed to believe made little or no difference in the way they lived. They had a popular form of godliness (reputation), but there was no moral or spiritual power (character) in it. Religion prospered while the sins of the nation deepened and God's judgment ripened. As long as the people supported the temple ministry and gave lip service to the faith of their fathers, nothing else was demanded of them; but Jeremiah called for something deeper.

The manager of a Christian radio station phoned me to complain about something I had said in a radio message. "If I understand you," he said, "you claim that if people are saved, there will be a change in their lives and you'll be able to see the evidence of salvation."

"Yes," I replied, "that's what I teach." Then I quoted 2 Corinthians 5:17: "Therefore, if anyone is in Christ, he is a new creation; old things have passed away; behold, all things have become new."

"Well, if you keep that up, we're going to drop your program!"

"Why would you do that?" I asked. "Don't you believe that God's people should be different from the unsaved crowd?"

"But a Christian can be carnal," he argued, "and a carnal Christian looks and acts just like an unsaved person. What about Lot? And how about the 'wood, hay, and straw' of 1 Corinthians 3:12?"

I tried to explain that Christians who deliberately disobey God eventually are chastened by the Lord, and that 1 John teaches that saved people don't habitually practice sin; but it was a lost cause. I hung up feeling frustrated that anybody would oppose messages that exhorted believers to practice godly, separated Christian living.

Vance Havner described the church accurately: "We are

challenged these days, but not changed; convicted, but not converted. We hear, but do not; and thereby we deceive ourselves."[2]

There is another parallel between our day and Jeremiah's: it was a time when religion was "big business" and the temple ministry was prospering. The priests and false prophets peddled a popular brand of religion that gave the people enough experience to make them happy but not enough truth to make them holy. They could worship Baal one day and then go to the temple the next day to worship Jehovah, and nobody was apt to criticize them, even though Baal worshipers were allowed to murder their own children. If that sounds pagan, just remember that in the United States, we have an annual slaughter of 1.5 million babies in the womb, and many religious people endorse it.

What did Jehovah think of all this? Jeremiah cried,

> An astonishing and horrible thing
> Has been committed in the land:
> The prophets prophesy falsely,
> And the priests rule by their own power;
> And My people love to have it so (5:30–31).

The nation was destroyed "Because of the sins of her prophets / And the iniquities of her priests" (Lam. 4:13). Jeremiah has recorded for us the names of some of the "spiritual leaders" of his day. Their chief was Pashhur (see Jer. 20:1ff.), a priest who ran the temple ministry and did all he could to silence Jeremiah. One day he slapped Jeremiah in the face and then put him in the stocks. Another leader was Hananiah, who told people that Jeremiah's sermons were all lies (see Jer. 28:1ff.). A third was Shemaiah, who wrote slanderous letters against Jeremiah (see Jer. 29:24ff.). Ahab and Zedekiah were two exiled prophets in Babylon, and they preached to the captive Jews a message of false hope (see 29:21).

These five men, plus many other false prophets and hypocritical priests, were popular with the people. Why? Because they dealt only with surface matters and never dared to get down to the root of the problem—the desperate need for repentance.

> They have also healed the hurt of
>   My people slightly,
> Saying, "Peace, peace!"
> When there is no peace (Jer. 6:14).

When the diagnosis is wrong, how can the remedy be right? I agree with Eugene Peterson: "The task of the prophet is not to smoothe things over but to make things right."[3]

Please don't get the idea that these temple ministers openly denounced the faith. No, they used the right language and appealed to the name of the Lord; but it was all counterfeit. The Lord said, "I have heard what the prophets have said who prophesy lies in My name, saying, 'I have dreamed, I have dreamed!' How long will this be in the heart of the prophets who prophesy lies? Indeed they are prophets of the deceit of their own heart" (23:25–26). Their messages did not come from the Lord, but still they claimed that their dreams and visions were authentic; and the people believed them.

After the fall of Jerusalem, Jeremiah wrote,

> Your prophets have seen for you
> False and deceptive visions;
> They have not uncovered your iniquity,
> To bring back your captives,
> But have envisioned for you false
>   prophecies and delusions (Lam. 2:14).

These men thought they were filled with the Spirit when they were only fooled by the spirits. In their duplicity, they had turned the light into darkness.

They used the familiar theological language, which made their messages even more dangerous. They assured the people that judgment would never come to Judah because God was on their side. To begin with, the temple of the Lord was there, and God would never permit His house to be destroyed by godless Gentiles! Furthermore, the nation had the Law of God, the rite of circumcision, and the security of the holy covenant; and these things made them special to Jehovah. Their properly ordained priesthood was busy in the temple, offering daily the assigned sacrifices and prayers; and the ark of the covenant was safely enshrined in the Holy of Holies. The worshipers were bringing their tithes and offerings, and the budget was being met. What more could a nation need?

Only one thing: repentance. But the word *repent* was not in the vocabulary of the popular preachers. Their key word was *peace,* and their message was that Jehovah was at the beck and call of His chosen people. To quote Eugene Peterson again: "Religion was supernatural assistance to do whatever you wished: make money, insure a good harvest, feel good, murder the person you hate, get ahead of your neighbor."[4] Does that sound familiar?

As in Jeremiah's day, so today, people are willing to be led astray and to support and defend the very people who deceive and destroy them. "My people love to have it so" (Jer. 5:31). Why? Because human nature wants to take the easy path that avoids having to hear God's Word, repent, and obey God's will. That's why the crowd follows Pashhur rather than Jeremiah, chooses Barabbas instead of Jesus, and still stones the true prophets and scourges God's servants. The crowd wants the broad road; it's easier, it's quicker, and there's a lot more company.

Speaking about the people who "love to have it so," Joseph Parker said, "They do not prize Scriptural teaching. They want to hear something fresh, racy, piquant, startling. They do not sit, Bible in hand, testing the speaker by the revelation; and what they ask for they get. They ask for chaff, and they get it."[5]

At least sixty-six times in his prophecy, Jeremiah wrote about the heart. "The heart is deceitful above all things, / And desperately wicked; / Who can know it?" (17:9). To a nation caught up in shallow, external religion, God called through His prophet, "And you will seek Me and find Me, when you search for Me with all your heart" (29:13). At least nine times, Jeremiah wrote about the imagination of man's evil heart. Pashhur and his crowd never preached surgical sermons like that. They promised peace, protection, and prosperity; and the crowds applauded and supported them.

Jehovah watched as His people went astray, and He said,

> For My people have committed two evils:
> They have forsaken Me, the fountain
>   of living waters,
> And hewn themselves cisterns—
>   broken cisterns that can hold no
>   water (Jer. 2:13).

That message wasn't too popular, and eventually it got Jeremiah into trouble with the "in crowd" of the religious establishment. But he was a shepherd, not a hireling; and he didn't quit, even though the people rejected his ministry.

One last parallel between our day and Jeremiah's day: the false prophets were covetous men who used religion for personal gain. They gloried in their own prosperity and in the prosperity of the temple and the nation. After all, were they not God's chosen people, and was not their wealth proof of their faithfulness and of God's blessing? (It is interesting to note that *Pashhur* means "surrounded with prosperity.")

Jeremiah dared to preach about the tenth commandment:

> Because from the least of them even
>   to the greatest of them,
> Everyone is given to covetousness;
> And from the prophet even to the priest,
> Everyone deals falsely (6:13 and 8:10).

> Yet your eyes and your heart are for nothing but your covetousness (22:17).

When a person is covetous, he is in danger of breaking *all* the commandments; "for the love of money is a root of all kinds of evil" (1 Tim. 6:10). Once someone starts coveting, he may stoop to lying, stealing, even murdering, to get what he wants.

Money and ministry have been in conflict in the church ever since Ananias and Sapphira lied about the sale of their real estate (see Acts 5) and Simon Magus tried to buy from Peter the power of imparting the gift of the Holy Spirit (see Acts 8:14–24). "Not greedy for money" is a requirement for both elders and deacons in the church (see 1 Tim. 3:3, 8; Titus 1:7). In his farewell address to the Ephesian elders, Paul reminded them that he had worked hard to pay his bills and had not coveted anyone's wealth (see Acts 20:33–35).

Of all the New Testament writers, Peter and Jude have given us the strongest denunciations of the hucksters who use religion for the purpose of making money: "By covetousness they will exploit you with deceptive words. . . . They have a heart trained in covetous practices, and are accursed children" (2 Pet. 2:3, 14). Peter compared them to Balaam "who loved the wages of unrighteousness" (2:15), and Jude echoed his warning: "They . . . have run greedily in the error of Balaam for profit" (v. 11). Jude also warned that "they mouth great swelling words, flattering people to gain advantage" (v. 16).

In recent months, it has been interesting to watch various organizations rush for shelter in order to convince people of their financial integrity. Certainly there is nothing wrong with legitimate accrediting agencies (the ministry I direct helped to found one), but there is more to financial integrity than a *bona fide* board and a certified audit. *Methods* of raising funds are important, and so are *motives*. Some schemes for supporting the gospel are unworthy of the gospel. Paul testified, "For neither at any time did we use flattering words, as you know, nor a cloak for covetousness—God is witness" (1 Thess. 2:5). J. B. Phillips paraphrases it, "No one could ever say, as again you know, that we used flattery to conceal greedy motives, and God himself is our witness."

God is also a witness to *dis*honesty as well as honesty, and when He finds it, He judges it.

If our day is like Jeremiah's day (and I believe it is,) we are living in a day of reproach. We are also living in a day when God is about to judge His people. "For the time has come for judgment to begin at the house of God" (1 Pet. 4:17). It is a sobering truth that *God would rather destroy His temple and encourage His Holy City than permit His leaders to promote religious duplicity and His people to support it.* He waited for decades before sending His judgment, and He repeatedly sent His messengers to warn His people; but His people did not listen. At least eleven times in Jeremiah's prophecy, the Lord said to the nation: "I spoke to you, rising up early" (7:13, 25; 11:7; 25:3–4; 26:5;

29:19; 32:33; 35:14–15; 44:4). The Hebrew word translated "rising up early" means "persistently," "diligently." God kept after them! But His people preferred the broken cisterns to the living waters.

The blighting influence of the false prophets spread across the land until almost everybody was affected by it. Again, listen to God's words through Jeremiah:

> I have seen a horrible thing in
>   the prophets of Jerusalem:
> They commit adultery and walk in lies;
> They also strengthen the hands of evildoers,
> So that no one turns back from his wickedness.
> All of them are like Sodom to Me,
> And her inhabitants like Gomorrah. . . . For from the
>   prophets of Jerusalem
> Profaneness has gone out into all the land (Jer. 23:
>   14–15).

The Hebrew word translated "profaneness" means "to act falsely," "to act with hypocrisy." You can also translate it "godlessness," "defilement," "moral depravity," "corruption," "pollution." No wonder there are so many scandals in our land today when the land is so infected with moral and spiritual pollution!

In his memorable sermon "The Method of Grace," based on Jeremiah 6:14 ("They have also healed the hurt of My people slightly, / Saying, 'Peace, peace!' / When there is no peace"), George Whitefield said:

> As God can send a nation or people no greater blessing than to give them faithful, sincere, and upright ministers, so the greatest curse that God can possibly send upon a people in this world is to give them over to blind,

unregenerate, carnal, lukewarm, and unskilled guides. And yet, in all ages, we find that there have been many wolves in sheep's clothing . . . that prophesied smoother things than God did allow.[6]

And, alas, His people love to have it so.

4
REVIEW

The first step down for any church is taken when it surrenders its high opinion of God.

A.W. TOZER

Raphael was painting his famous Vatican frescoes when a couple of cardinals stopped by to watch and criticize.

"The face of the apostle Paul is too red," said one.

Raphael replied, "He blushes to see into whose hands the church has fallen."

Jeremiah would have identified with that reply. "Were they ashamed when they had committed abomination?" he asked. Then he answered, "No! They were not at all ashamed; / Nor did they know how to blush" (6:15 and 8:12).

Why did the people of Judah unblushingly accept and support a religious system that dethroned the very God who had made them great? Jeremiah explained why it happened: "The heart is deceitful above all things, / And desperately wicked; / Who can know it?" (17:9). In other words, the heart of the problem is the problem of the heart; and you and I have that same kind of heart. The setting and the script may be different, but the players haven't changed since Jeremiah's day.

The people of Judah followed their hearts and plunged headlong into a false religion that promised them what they wanted. Their leaders followed their hearts and yielded to those inner cravings that lurk in all of us, cravings for power, wealth, and popularity. These men may not have seen themselves as false prophets, but that's what they were just the same. They may have been sincere as they shared their dreams and announced their visions, but they were still leading the people astray. When they persecuted Jeremiah, they no doubt thought they were doing God a service.

Seeing that their hearts were bent on evil, God sent a "strong delusion, that they should believe the lie" (2 Thess. 2:11), because the penalty for rejecting truth is accepting lies. The greatest judgment God can send on His people is letting them have their own way: "And He gave them their request, / But sent leanness into their soul" (Ps. 106:15). The success of Josiah's reformation left behind just the right atmosphere for the leaven of hypocrisy to develop, and it grew rapidly.

I believe that the church's present integrity crisis is partly the result of the false success of the evangelical movement in recent years. That's a radical statement, I know, but I think it can be defended. In a perceptive book that is more relevant today than when it was published in 1980, Jon Johnston writes, "Current evangelical popularity presents powerful pressures to compromise biblical values for the sake of social acceptance." Then he adds, "Our degree of compromise has reached epidemic proportions."[1]

What some people in the church consider "success" is to others the judgment of God. He is letting us have our own way, and we are starting to discover that our assets are really liabilities. George MacDonald said, "In whatever man does without God, he must fail miserably *or succeed more miserably*" (italics mine). Ponder that statement, and then consider what the Lord said through Malachi to the religious leaders of his day:

> "And now, O priests, this
>   commandment is for you.
> If you will not hear,
> And if you will not take it to heart,
> To give glory to My name,"
> Says the LORD of hosts,
> "I will send a curse upon you,
> And I will curse your blessings.
> Yes, I have cursed them already,
> Because you do not take it to heart" (Mal. 2:1–2).

To *take away blessings* would be judgment enough; but for God to *turn blessings into curses* is a judgment terrible to consider. Imagine people being so blind to God's will that they actually rejoice over things that will eventually destroy them! But when God's people stop glorifying Him, He must judge their sin. "For there is no partiality with God" (Rom. 2:11). "The LORD will judge His people" (Heb. 10:30). When individuals value the gift more than the Giver, the gift becomes an idol, and they start to worship and serve "the creature rather than the Creator" (Rom. 1:25).

Idolatry means living on substitutes, and the God whose name is Jealous (see Exod. 34:14) simply will not tolerate them. Let's consider some of the "evangelical substitutes" that have been robbing the church of her integrity. But I must warn you: some of the things I'll mention are so much a part of our modern Christian way of life that you may be shocked and even offended at the list. Please be patient; it's all a part of the diagnosis.

At the top of the list, I think, is the church's desire to be accepted and approved by the world in general and "important people" in particular. In recent years, we have sought the applause of men, not the approval of God, and too many ministries have depended on "Christian celebrities" to get the attention and support of God's people. It used to be that the three most important things for success in our meetings were that people be filled with the Spirit, burdened for souls, and ready to give God the glory. But then it became necessary to have famous people on the program, such as Hollywood stars, prominent athletes, and well-known entertainers, all of whom were expected to say a good word for God. It's doubtful that all these famous people were really saved. They were probably only using our organizations to promote themselves, and now we can look back and count the casualties.

A. W. Tozer called this the "Wheaties approach" to evangelism: just as you should eat Wheaties because John Jones eats Wheaties, so you should be a Christian because John Jones is a Christian. This approach is ideal for a society like ours that worships success and has confidence in testimonials. However, when the emphasis is on the fame of the witness, not his or her faith in Christ, something is bound to go wrong; and it has. We've discovered that these people were only celebrities to admire, not heroes to follow, and that the way they lived too often contradicted what they said. Yes, we're embarrassed; but we have nobody to blame but ourselves.

Basically, it was a problem of integrity: reputation was more important than character, and popularity and the ability to draw a crowd were more important than a consistent, Christian lifestyle. And that approach led to things starting to come apart at the seams. It was a subtle form of religious pragmatism: it's working; therefore, God must be blessing it. As long as we catch fish, what difference does it make what kind of hooks or bait we use?

For a while, Hollywood stars and athletes were featured, but then the politicians moved in. How thrilled the church was when well-known preachers were invited to the White House! How exciting it was that men and women in high offices quoted the Bible or told the press they were born again! For some of them, the testimony was true, and we thank God for their witness; but for too many others, it was just another way to get the attention of the Christian public and harvest more votes. The "Religious Right" was a force the politicians had to reckon with; and "if you can't whip 'em, join 'em" seemed to become a policy as well as a platitude.

When television came along, the Wheaties approach got a new lease on life. Television is basically an entertainment medium, and that's what the Wheaties approach really is—entertainment. The religious leader with the right kind of charisma had it made, because the viewing audience was all prepared for him. The Christian public had become so accustomed to religious entertainment, celebrities, and "pop" gospel that the transition was easy. We had created a powerful monster with a ravenous appetite, and we had to feed it. The church had its own personality cult that rivaled anything Hollywood could offer; and millions of people were willing to support it and call it "God's blessing."

Now God seems to have turned the blessing into a curse.

Once you make "getting results" your chief aim, there is no end to the mistakes you will make; and believe me, we made them. First you worry about numbers. Then you start substituting statistical records for spiritual reality, which is something like reading the recipe instead of eating the meal.

How many attended? How many made decisions? How many joined? How much was given in the offering? All these things were more important than whether or not we glorified God in the meeting. Before long, the church ceased to be seen as people in an assembly: it became names and numbers in a file and, later, in a computer. People were not an end in themselves; they became a means to an end—getting a bigger crowd and getting more results.

Let me hasten to say that there is nothing unspiritual about keeping accurate records. Spurgeon claimed that those who criticized statistics usually had none to report, and I think he was right. One day at a pastors' meeting, I was piously attacking church statistics when Dr. Walter L. Wilson said to me, "Young man, there is a book in the Bible called Numbers!" The good doctor was right; but he would be the first to agree with me that there is a significant difference between knowing the number of the sheep and knowing the state of the flock. The good shepherd is concerned about even one sheep that has strayed away.

This emphasis on statistics soon created an atmosphere of competition in the church. Who had the biggest church? Who had the biggest Sunday school? Unfortunately, the competition sometimes led to deception, until finally our contests were called off because of rain: the statistics were all wet.

Publishers jumped on the bandwagon and offered books telling us how *any* pastor could increase church and Sunday school attendance by doing what the experts were doing in the megachurches. (That's a new word we had to coin to keep up with our success.) We could also hear these men in person by attending their schools or seminars.

I certainly have no case against learning from the other fellow. After all, why reinvent the wheel? But I do have a case against any philosophy that turns ministry into mechanics and hands me a book of formulas that are guaranteed to succeed. I also have a problem with publishers that sign up "famous men" to write these books but don't first find out whether or not these surefire methods are based on good theology. If the medical profession followed this approach, we'd all be dead.

Sometimes as I page through a Christian publication and look at the news and advertising, it almost makes me nauseous. The gospel has become big business, and all sorts of strange birds are perched in the branches. Our personality cult has gone full circle, and now we are promoting ministry and merchandise the way the world promotes toothpaste and used cars. The only thing more sickening than reading one of these magazines is visiting the exhibition hall of the average Christian convention, seeing the people and merchandise in living color, and watching as they compete for business.

Where did we go wrong? Again, it was a matter of integrity: *we substituted "getting results" for bearing fruit to the glory of God.* Almost anyone can manufacture results, but fruit has to flow from life. "Without Me you can do nothing" (John 15:5). We replaced an integer with a fraction when we separated ministry from the very Source of its power—almighty God. We made it easy for people to be "successful" in Christian work as long as they had talent and could get a crowd. It wasn't important to be holy. It was important to have a great press release.

Saintly Robert Murray McCheyne said, "It is not great talents God blesses so much as great likeness to Jesus."[2] I wish I had known that sooner; and now that I know it, I need to heed it more.

A subtle change took place: many churches almost ceased to be congregations assembled to worship God and became audiences gathered together to watch men. Believers who used

46

to be participants in sacred liturgy became spectators at a religious performance. "Sanctuaries" dedicated to the worship of God became "auditoriums" where the goats laughed and the sheep languished. We began to worship what A. W. Tozer called "the Great God Entertainment."

Of course, this approach only strengthened the weaknesses we had already created: the personality cult, the lust for statistics, and the marketing of the faith. With the arrival of television, religious entertainers found the ideal medium for spreading their gospel of good feelings. This is not to suggest that everybody who has used or is using television for ministry is either a fraud or a failure. Some of my best friends are in religious TV, but I can't say that everybody in the medium has escaped the Great God Entertainment. I'll explain why in a later chapter.

I'm convinced that everything the church is supposed to do in this world is a by-product of spiritual worship, and that includes evangelism, missions, giving, works of mercy, education, and personal holiness and service. First God calls us to worship, then He sends us out to witness and to work. God wants worship to come first, for only then will we be energized by His power and bring glory to His name. Worship puts God where He deserves to be and keeps man where he ought to be. But in the worship of the Great God Entertainment, man gets the glory, and God gets lost in the fun.

If this analysis is correct, it's obvious that the church has been losing its integrity for a long time. We've been living on substitutes and didn't know it, or perhaps didn't want to admit it. We've divorced ministry from worship, witness from character, and duty from doctrine; and we've done all this to be popular and get results instead of to bear fruit to the glory of God. The media scandals have certainly caused problems;

but even more, they have *revealed* problems, problems that for many years have been spreading in the church like a deadly infection. Now the infection has appeared for everybody to see.

Long before the scandals broke, other symptoms were telling us that something was wrong in the body. For one thing, the church was just too popular with the world and was starting to depend more on political influence than on preaching and prayer. We no longer confronted the world the way Moses confronted Pharaoh or John the Baptist confronted Herod. We stopped being ambassadors and became diplomats, and then bragged about our acceptance by famous people.

The growth of church budgets and crowds apparently made little difference in society at large or, for that matter, in the Christian home. Divorce increased and even invaded the church and the ministry. Popular Christian personalities could become involved in marital mix-ups, with no evidence of repentance, and still have a following that would applaud their performances and buy their books and records. Yet with all our impressive statistics, we have hardly taken a "baby step" toward helping society deal with narcotics abuse, crime, family problems, and sexual immorality. The fear of AIDS is probably changing more lifestyles than is the fear of God.

This chapter has been negative, so let me balance things by making it clear that I don't consider the post-World War II era of the church a time of total defeat and failure. Quite the contrary: it was a time of excitement and expansion, and I thank God that I've been permitted to live and minister during such eventful years. What a thrilling picture future historians will give us when they finally put all the pieces together and tell us what really happened!

But there was so much going on that we didn't see the problems developing, and now we're paying for it. In response to new ideas and challenges, many ministries grew so rapidly that we didn't take time to examine things carefully. Whenever the Holy Spirit plants the true seed, the enemy plants the counterfeit; and it's not until later that we see the difference.

Nor am I suggesting that all of us who ministered during this era are personally to blame for the scandals that have shamed the church. However, I feel that many of us probably helped to create the atmosphere that allowed this thing to happen. Perhaps we did it innocently because we didn't know any better, or if we knew, we didn't care to rock the boat. It was too easy to follow the people who believed in the "new philosophy" of ministry, people who were leading us from one victory to another. True, now and then we could hear distant voices warning us of our folly; but who pays attention to sirens when you don't smell any smoke? Anyway, hindsight always has 20/20 vision.

But now that we know, maybe we should face things honestly and ask God to forgive us.

"The last word of our Lord to the church is not the Great Commission," said Vance Havner. "The Great Commission is indeed our program to the end of the age, but our Lord's last word to the church is 'Repent.' "[3]

We should be blushing.

We should be repenting.

Perhaps the prayer of Ezra will help us get started:

> O my God, I am too ashamed and humiliated to lift up my face to You, my God; for our iniquities have risen higher than our heads, and our guilt has grown up to the heavens (Ezra 9:6).

5
RESPONSIBILITY

There is nothing attractive about the Gospel
to the natural man;
the only man who finds the Gospel attractive
is the man who is convicted of sin.

OSWALD CHAMBERS

The news media have had a great deal to say about preachers and money, and preachers and morals; but not much has been said about the real problem: preachers and the message. The only person I've heard mention this theological issue is Chuck Colson in an address he gave at the Christian Booksellers Convention in 1987. He made a similar statement in his book *Kingdoms of Conflict*. This is what he wrote:

> The effect of preaching a false theology can be disastrous. Most attribute the fall of Jim and Tammy Bakker to greed, sexual indiscretion, or the corruption of power. These were, of course, serious contributing factors. But the root cause of their downfall was that for years the Bakkers had preached a false gospel of material advancement. . . . Tragically, the Bakkers deluded themselves into believing their own false message.[1]

As Chuck was speaking that evening, I opened my Bible to 1 Thessalonians 2:3–5, and I read:

> For our exhortation did not come from error or uncleanness, nor was it in deceit. But as we have been approved by God to be entrusted with the gospel, even so we speak, not as pleasing men, but God who tests our hearts. For neither at any time did we use flattering words, as you know, nor a cloak for covetousness—God is witness.

God's servants are divinely appointed stewards who are "entrusted with the gospel." This is a great privilege, but it is also a solemn responsibility. "Moreover it is required in stewards that one be found faithful" (1 Cor. 4:2). This faithfulness involves at least three elements that must be right: the *message* ("our exhortation did not come from error"), the *motive* ("or uncleanness"), and the *method* ("nor was it in deceit"). Let's consider these three elements and see how they relate to the integrity crisis.

The message must be right, and that message is the gospel of Jesus Christ, the gospel of the grace of God. There is but one gospel, and it centers in the death, burial, and resurrection of Jesus Christ. The gospel (good news) is "that Christ died for our sins according to the Scriptures, and that He was buried, and that He rose again the third day according to the Scriptures" (1 Cor. 15:3–4). Sinners who repent and trust in Jesus Christ are forgiven and receive from God the gift of eternal life (see 1 John 5:10–13).

God is so jealous over this message that He declares "accursed" anybody who preaches another "gospel" (see Gal. 1:6–9). Those who change this message by adding to it, taking from it, or perverting it are false teachers who are unfaithful to the Lord and in danger of His judgment. Their message comes "from error."

The modern "success gospel" is perfectly suited to a society like ours that worships health, wealth, and happiness. The people who preach this gospel dip here and there into the Old Testament to pull out their proof texts, but they willfully reject "the whole counsel of God" (Acts 20:27). The success gospel is a cheap message for people who are looking for a "quick fix" for their lives but not a permanent change in their character. A. W. Tozer said it best: "It appears that too many Christians want to enjoy the thrill of feeling right but are not willing to endure the inconvenience of being right."[2]

Why is God so concerned that we preach the right message? Because God believes in integrity, and a false gospel destroys integrity. To begin with, the message of the gospel is vitally related to the very nature of God. Jesus does not simply save; He *is* the Savior. When we change the message of God, we change the God of the message. The God of the "success" preachers is not the God of the Bible or of the historic church. He is a manufactured god, an idol; and as A. W. Tozer has reminded us, "The essence of idolatry is the entertainment of thoughts about God that are unworthy of Him."[3]

The pop gospel of success tries to make us believe that God's greatest concern is to make us happy, not to make us holy, and that He is more concerned about the physical and the material than He is the moral and the spiritual. The "success god" is a celestial errand boy whose only responsibility is to respond to our every call and make sure that we are enjoying life.

As I listen to these preachers, some questions come to mind: Where in their theology is the God of Abraham, who was told to sacrifice his only son? Where is the God of Isaac, who was willing to put himself on the altar? Where is the God of Jacob, whose sons brought him grief and shame? Where is the God of Moses, who was kept out of the Promised Land because he robbed God of glory? Where is the God of the apostles, who were arrested and beaten and finally killed because they wouldn't keep quiet about Jesus? Where is the God of our Lord Jesus Christ, who suffered as no one has ever suffered, "Smitten by God, and afflicted" (Isa. 53:4)?

I don't find this God in their preaching. Why? Because He doesn't fit their message. They have a gospel without integrity, a fraction of a message, divorced from the very God they claim to represent. A partial gospel is no gospel at all, for there can be no good news when God has been left out.

My late "boss," Theodore H. Epp, attended a convention at which a popular success preacher was one of the featured speakers. Mr. Epp wanted to hear this famous man in person; so, Bible in hand, he went to the meeting.

Imagine his surprise when he heard the speaker say (and here I paraphrase): "You will notice that I don't have a Bible. I've stopped using a Bible in the pulpit. People don't want sermons; they want to hear what God means to us in our own lives."

So grieved was Mr. Epp that he left the hall, went to his room, fell on his knees, and asked God to forgive him for attending that meeting, and even for attending the convention! He packed his things, checked out and went back home.

"Our job isn't to give the people what they want," he used to say to me. "Our job is to give them what they need *but try to make them want it*." To him, teaching the "word of truth" was the main thing.

The success gospel not only presents a distorted view of God, it perverts the biblical doctrine of the Person and work of Jesus Christ. God has every right to pronounce judgment on those who preach a false gospel, *because the message of the gospel cost Him His Son!* Jesus shed His blood to satisfy the holy law of God so that lost sinners might be forgiven and reconciled to God. Jesus didn't die to make us healthy, wealthy, and happy; He died to make us holy. To turn Calvary into a sanctified credit card that gives us the privilege of a hedonistic shopping spree is to cheapen the most costly thing God ever did.

We've noted that God's ultimate goal in history is to "gather together in one all things in Christ" (Eph. 1:10). Then and only then will our bodies be fully redeemed and delivered from the burdens of this life. God's goal for each of us *personally* is that we might "be conformed to the image of His Son" (Rom. 8:29). He wants to make us like Jesus, and He starts that process the instant we are born into His family. As we grow in the Christian life, we "are being transformed into the same image from glory to glory, just as by the Spirit of the Lord" (2 Cor. 3:18).

But the success preachers don't see conformity to Christ as the goal of the Christian life. It surely must embarrass them when they have to face the fact that, according to their message, Jesus was not a success. He was not wealthy, and He spent His life identified with the poor and the outcasts. He was a "Man of sorrows and acquainted with grief" (Isa. 53:3), not a celebrity enjoying a life of extravagance. I may be wrong, but I believe that if Jesus were on earth today, He would condemn the extravagant and flamboyant lifestyle of these success preachers and their disciples. In His life and ministry, in His teachings, and especially in His death, Jesus Christ repudiates the success gospel.

The success preachers give us a distorted view of God, of the Savior, of the Christian life, and also of the church. According to them, the church of Jesus Christ is a gathering of happy people who are enjoying life. According to my Bible, the church is a gathering of hurting people who are seeking to be holy before God and helpful to a needy world. Yes, there ought to be celebration and joy when the church meets to worship; but there must also be the sharing of burdens, the washing of wounds, and the healing of broken hearts. But according to the success gospel, Christians shouldn't be hurting at all!

The church is a family that comes together for encouragement, spiritual nourishment, and discipline. It's an army that assembles to be equipped for battle and to hear God's marching orders. It's a flock that seeks God's protection in a dangerous world, a bride that expresses devotion to the heavenly Bridegroom, a group of servants that seek their Master's will. We meet together, not to escape life, but to be equipped and encouraged to go back to life with its burdens and battles. Yes, we have our times of happiness, but that's not our primary goal. Our goals are holiness and helpfulness; happiness is only a by-product.

When the church preaches the wrong message, it tears things apart, and the ministry loses its integrity. We can't divorce our message from what God is, what God did at Calvary, what God is doing in the world today, and what God will do in the future. But that's just what the success hucksters have done. Once you manufacture your own gospel, it isn't long before you start practicing it, *and then you begin to lose your integrity*.

Recall the process described in 1 John 1:5–10. First, you lie to others and stop practicing the truth (v. 6). The you start lying to yourself, and you lose the truth (v. 8). Finally, you begin lying to God and making Him a liar; and as a result, you lose His Word (v. 10). John made it clear that ministry involves integrity and that you must not separate the messenger and the message. When you do, both the messenger and the message lose their integrity.

But it isn't enough to preach the right message; we must also preach with the right motives. "For our exhortation did not come from . . . uncleanness" (1 Thess. 2:3). The New International Version of the Bible translates it "from impure motives." Paul didn't major on pleasing men so that he could become a popular preacher, nor did he exploit people so that he could become a rich preacher. His basic motive for ministry was to please God, and that's what kept him going. He knew that God was constantly testing his heart to see if his motives were pure.

In *Walden,* Henry David Thoreau wrote, "There is no odor so bad as that which arises from goodness tainted."[4] And few things taint our goodness like covetousness, a desire to be popular, and the ecstatic feeling that comes when we exercise power over the people who give us their idolatrous adoration. When our motives are wrong, our ministry is wrong; and the consequences are tragic for us, for those who follow us, and for the whole church.

It's probably impossible for anybody in this life to minister from absolutely pure motives, but by the grace of God, we can try. When we find ourselves resisting criticism and cultivating praise, we know something is wrong. When we really start to believe all the good things people say about us, we're in danger. If our hearts are right before God, praise ought to humble us, not inflate us.

In recent years, the church has had too many celebrities and not enough servants, too many people with plenty of medals but no scars. To look at their lives and listen to their messages, you would never know that the gospel was about a humble Jew who was poor, rejected, and crucified; nor would you ever suspect that He said, "Blessed are you poor, / For yours is the kingdom of God" (Luke 6:20), or "But woe to you who are rich, / For you have received your consolation"

(Luke 6:24). A religious celebrity manufactures the message that will most enhance his popularity and perhaps increase his income. A true servant is concerned about integrity, both his personal integrity and the integrity of his message.

In a later chapter, I'll have more to say about the dangers of money and power in the ministry. Let's move on to Paul's third concern: our methods must be right.

There is no place for "deceit" in the ministry of the gospel. Deceit can have no rightful place in the promotion of the gospel. Fraud and faith just don't go together. I've heard sincere Christians say, "I don't care what your methods are, just as long as your message is right!" They should stop to consider the fundamental fact that the message helps to determine the method. *Some methods of gospel ministry are unworthy of the gospel.* The Greek word translated "deceit" means "to bait a hook." In all his dealings with people, Paul was open and honest. He didn't try to "catch" them with "bait" so he could "hook" them with the gospel.

A friend of mine once served on the staff of a church pastored by a popular success preacher. I asked him why his boss didn't preach about sin, repentance, or judgment.

"Because he knows that most people won't listen to that kind of preaching," my friend replied. "He 'baits' them with his success sermons, and then the staff does personal work behind the scenes to make sure the people understand the gospel."

I don't find that kind of evangelism anywhere in the ministry of Jesus, His disciples, or the early church. Jesus sometimes used an interesting image to get people's attention, but He always confronted them with their sins. He won the attention of the woman at the well by talking about "living water," but eventually He got her to face her sins: "Go, call your husband, and come here" (John 4:16). Jesus was far from being a success preacher. In fact, some of His messages were so convicting that His listeners wanted to kill Him!

Sermons that flatter sinners will never save sinners. I once heard an evangelist congratulate people for walking an aisle to meet with counselors; and when he did, he contradicted the very gospel he preached. True gospel preaching exalts God and condemns the lost sinner; it doesn't encourage the sinner's pride. If anything, man's sinful ego needs to be broken before a holy God; and that's what the message of the gospel does. Before we can believe the good news about Jesus, we must accept the bad news about ourselves.

Flattery has been defined as "manipulation, not communication." When we start manipulating people instead of ministering to them, we cease to be faithful stewards of the gospel, and we rob people of the opportunity of making responsible decisions for Jesus Christ. Jesus and Paul *persuaded* people; they didn't seduce them, coerce them, or exploit them. The gospel strips away the sinner's ability to save himself, but it never takes away his responsibility to obey God's commands.

Flattery is only one device that preachers use to bait the hook to catch their unwary fish. Another trick is *offering simple answers to very complex problems*. The preacher who shouts, "Jesus is the answer!" is certainly making a valid statement. But he is doing about as much good as the physician who shouts to the folks in his waiting room, "Surgery is the answer!" This is pure demagoguery, even if it is backed up with a verse from the Bible.

Someone, perhaps Mark Twain, said that a lie runs around the world while truth is putting on her boots, and he was right. Fallen human nature wants to believe lies, especially "religious lies," which makes it easy for the demagogue to succeed. James Fenimore Cooper defined a *demagogue* as "one who advances his own interests by affecting a deep devotion to the interests of the people."⁵ Of all demagogues, the religious ones are the most despicable. They know how to bait the hook.

My wife and I had just checked into our motel in Orlando, Florida, when we were approached by a friendly young lady who offered us free transportation to Disney World and Epcot Center. My radar immediately went to work, and I asked, "And what do we have to do in return for this favor?" Then the truth came out: all we had to do was give up several hours of our vacation time to watch a movie and then visit a real estate development. Those land promoters knew how to bait the hook, but at least they were honest about it. That's more than I can say for some preachers.

It's unfortunate that many Christians, when they are exposed to a ministry, don't know how to think theologically and ask the right questions. They lack spiritual discernment, and they also lack confidence in the people who do have discernment. The faithful pastor who warns his flock about a questionable media minister is likely to hear, "Oh, you're just jealous of his success! You're afraid we'll start sending him money!"

When I was in my first weeks of ministry as senior pastor of the Moody Church in Chicago, I was surprised to have a longtime member ask me, "When will you invite ———— to speak here?" and he named a well-known media preacher whose theology and ethics I consider deplorable.

"Never," I replied. "I don't want people to think this church endorses either his message or his lifestyle."

"He'll draw a big crowd!"

"We're not here just to build a crowd," I said. "We're here to build a church. And he can't help us."

I didn't see that member very much in the years that followed. How tragic that he lacked the ability to detect a religious fraud when he saw one, even though all his life he had been privileged to hear some of the world's leading preachers and Bible teachers. And he wasn't willing to accept his pastor's assessment. Fortunately, he was an exception.

What we believe determines how we behave, and both determine what we become. If we believe the truth, the truth will sanctify us (see John 17:17) and set us free (see John 8:31–32). If we believe lies, we will gradually *become a lie* as we lose our integrity and begin to practice duplicity. It's a fundamental principle that we will become like the god we worship. If that god is false, we become false. "Those who make them [false gods] are like them; / So is everyone who trusts in them" (Ps. 115:8).

"Little children, keep yourselves from idols" (1 John 5:21).

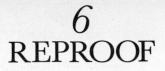

6
REPROOF

Preaching is indispensable to Christianity.
Without preaching, a necessary part
of its authenticity has been lost.
For Christianity is, in its very essence,
a religion of the Word of God.

JOHN R.W. STOTT

My conclusion is that the wrong kind of preachers have created the wrong kind of Christians by declaring the wrong kind of message, compelled by the wrong motives. So much for the diagnosis; now for the remedy. What kind of preachers do we need in the church today, and what kind of leaders?

Let's start with the preachers. The church today needs preachers like Jeremiah and John the Baptist.

It's interesting how much these two men have in common and how much we can learn from them. Both were born to be priests but called to be prophets. If I had my choice, I would rather be a priest than a prophet. After all, the work of a Jewish priest was routine. All he had to do was study the books of Moses and follow the regulations and schedules commanded by God. There were few surprises at the altar and not many opportunities to get in trouble with his people. He simply did the job he was assigned to do and went by the books.

But not so with the prophet! From one day to another, a prophet never knew what his ministry would be. He not only had to understand God's Word, but he also had to understand the people and the times in which he was living; and he had to know how to apply the changeless Word to his changing times. The priest could do his job and never pay attention to the news of the day, but not the prophet. He had to know what was going on! The priest was safe; the prophet was vulnerable. The priest could keep his mouth shut, but the prophet had to give God's message, whether the people wanted to hear it or not.

It takes courage to be a prophet. Both Jeremiah and John boldly confronted powerful men and hostile congregations as they declared God's truth; and both were killed because they were faithful to that truth. From the human point of view, both were failures.

Priestly ministry was not primarily a ministry of the Word, even though the priests were obligated to teach the people God's laws. The priests conducted a "formula" ministry. All they had to do was follow the rules written in their books and be careful that ceremony did not become ritual. Alas, too often it did!

The Old Testament priests dealt primarily with the *externals* of their religion, the sacrifices and washings, the diets and special days. But the prophets had to deal with the *internals*. They had to try to change the sinful human heart, and that's not easy to do. There was plenty of popular religion in Jeremiah's day and in John's day, but it didn't get to the hearts of the people.

A prophet has to be a radical and get to the root of every problem. (Our word *radical* comes from the Latin *radix,* which means "root.") That's why John the Baptist cried, "And even now the ax is laid to the root of the trees" (Matt. 3:10); and that's why Jeremiah denounced the false prophets who applied salve when they should have performed surgery (see Jeremiah 6:13–14). Had Jeremiah and John come as priests and not as prophets, the leaders might have accepted them; but because their ministries were prophetic, the leaders opposed them and eventually eliminated them.

The priest's main job was to preserve the past and protect the status quo. But the prophet's job was to interpret the present in the light of the past and then give guidance that would help guarantee the future. John and Jeremiah challenged the status quo, and they dared to announce that God was shaking things and getting ready to change things! People who want a comfortable religion don't respond gladly to that kind of message.

Because Jeremiah was a prophet of the heart, he looked beyond the externals of the Jewish religion and saw the deeper spiritual truths that were involved. The Jews revered their temple, but soon it would be destroyed (7:4–11). God would one day build a new temple that could not be destroyed. They gloried in their Law and their covenant, but God would make a new covenant that would be written on hearts and not on stones (see 31:31–34). In fact, the day would come when the precious ark of the covenant would be taken away and not even be missed (see 3:16–17), because God would be dwelling in His people in a new and living way. Even circumcision (see 4:4) and the sacrifices (see 7:21ff.) would be replaced by something spiritual and eternal and more wonderful.

To be sure, all these things had been blessings to the nation; but they were taking the place of the nation's faith in God. Jeremiah saw what the false prophets refused to see, that their blessings had become curses and would lead them to bondage: "Behold, you trust in lying words that cannot profit" (7:8).

63

If you want to learn how difficult it is for some people to give up the "furniture" of their faith and make room for something new, just get involved in a building program, or try to move an adult Sunday school class to a different room.

In our first pastorate, the Lord led us to tear down the church building and build a new edifice. Being young and zealous, I thought the people would rejoice; but not all of them did. The fact that the building was made of corrugated metal (Please, Lord, don't let it rain!), was totally inadequate, and was very suspect to the city building authorities didn't influence the minority. Until the day the wrecking crew arrived, I still heard them pray, "Thank You, Lord, for our little church!"

As I look back, I realize that a great many precious memories were wrapped up in that little tin building—weddings, funerals, people getting saved—but I wish the minority had looked ahead instead of looking back. The experience gave me my first introduction to the difference between being a priest and being a prophet.

A few years ago, while reading through Jeremiah's prophecy, I made a list of some pictures he gave of his ministry, and it helped me better understand the kind of ministry that the church needs but doesn't always want. Here's what Jeremiah was:

A destroyer, a builder, and a planter
See, I have this day set you over the
    nations and over the kingdoms,
To root out and to pull down,
To destroy and to throw down,
To build and to plant (1:10).

A city, a pillar, and a wall
For behold, I have made you this day

A fortified city and an iron pillar,
And bronze walls (1:18).

An assayer of metal and a fortress
I have set you as an assayer and a
    fortress among My people,
That you may know and test their way (6:27).

A physician
For the hurt of the daughter of my
    people I am hurt.
I am mourning;
Astonishment has taken hold of me.
Is there no balm in Gilead,
Is there no physician there?
Why then is there no recovery
For the health of the daughter of my people? (8:
    21–22).

A sacrifice
But I was like a docile lamb brought to the slaughter
    (11:19).

A runner
If you have run with the footmen,
    and they have wearied you,
Then how can you contend with horses? (12:5).

A shepherd
But if you will not hear it,
My soul will weep in secret for your pride;
My eyes will weep bitterly
And run down with tears,
Because the LORD's flock has been taken captive
    (13:17).

A troublemaker
Woe is me, my mother,

That you have borne me,
A man of strife and a man of
    contention to the whole earth! (15:10).

That last image bothers me: a troublemaker. Who wants to be a troublemaker? After I became senior pastor at the Moody Church, I discovered that prominent pulpits make preachers into good targets. All of my ministry, I had been accustomed to having "good press" and getting along well with the brethren, but then things changed.

I recall reading an article about myself and my ministry in a religious magazine and saying out loud, "Where did they get this? Not a bit of it is true!"

I phoned a good friend who knew something about battles with the brethren, and he said, "Don't worry about it. God forbid that they should approve of your ministry! I'd worry about you if they did! This is all new to you, but give yourself time. In a few years, you'll be where I am, and it won't hurt as much. They'll be shooting through the old holes!"

It was a tough lesson to learn: if you're faithful in your ministry, even some of your fellow preachers may not like it. But, my friend was right: they're shooting through the "old holes" now, and I hardly notice it.

John the Baptist could say a loud "Amen!" to each of these pictures, but I wonder if I can? I wonder how many who minister the Word can honestly say they have had this kind of ministry? If these pictures describe a true prophetic ministry, there are not many prophets today. The church is indeed a nonprophet organization.

Most people don't want a prophet around because a prophet makes them uncomfortable. A prophet weeps while others are laughing, and a prophet wears a yoke that gets in people's way and knocks expensive trinkets off the shelves.

While the complacent are monitoring religious conformity, the prophet is busy tearing down so he can build up, and rooting out so he can plant. While the popular leaders bend with the wind, the prophet stands as firm as a wall so he can lead the nation forward.

The false prophet is a peddler of cheap alloy, but the prophet is an assayer who turns on the heat so he can test the metal and take away the dross. He is a physician who exposes the ugly sores before he applies the medicine. He is, in short, a person who creates problems by revealing problems so that he can solve problems.

But while he's ministering, he's as vulnerable as a little lamb, as weary as a long-distance runner, and as broken-hearted as a loving shepherd who sees his flock scattered and exploited. He weeps so that we might have joy; he wears the yoke so that we might be set free.

John the Baptist knew what it meant to get discouraged in the ministry. When John was in Herod's prison, he sent some of his disciples to ask Jesus, "Are You the Coming One, or do we look for another?" (Matt. 11:3). Jesus sent John a gracious word of encouragement; and when John's disciples were out of earshot, He had this to say about him:

> What did you go out into the wilderness to see? A reed shaken by the wind? But what did you go out to see? A man clothed in soft garments? Indeed, those who wear soft clothing are in kings' houses. But what did you go out to see? A prophet? Yes, I say to you, and more than a prophet (Matt. 11:7–9).

John was not a *compromiser,* a "reed shaken by the wind." Like Jeremiah, he was a bronze wall and an iron pillar. He didn't let the attacks of men upset him or the applause of men influence him. Had John played along with the religious establishment, perhaps the leaders would have talked to Herod about freeing him; but John was the prisoner of conscience, not of Herod, and freedom on such terms would have meant the end of his ministry.

When religion is popular, popularity is the most important part of your religion, and you will have to compromise in order to maintain it. Jesus had that truth in mind when He said:

> But to what shall I liken this generation? It is like children sitting in the marketplaces and calling to their companions, and saying:
> > "We played the flute for you,
> > And you did not dance;
> > We mourned to you,
> > And you did not lament."
> For John came neither eating nor drinking, and they say, "He has a demon." The Son of Man came eating and drinking, and they say, "Look, a glutton and a winebibber, a friend of tax collectors and sinners!" (Matt. 11:16–19).

John was not a compromiser, nor was he a *celebrity*, enjoying rich clothes and elegant entertainments in kings' palaces. One of the weaknesses of the church in recent years has been the abundance of celebrities and the absence of servants. The way some media preachers have openly flaunted their extravagant lifestyle is a disgrace to them and to the church. However, few religious leaders have dared to criticize them or break fellowship with them. After all, when they attend the same conventions, share the same spotlights, and belong to the same influential committees, it's easy to ignore sin and call our cowardice "tolerance."

The church is not going to solve its integrity crisis until its ministers and members start to *live* the message of the gospel as well as *preach* it. The success preachers claim that an affluent lifestyle is a confirmation of the gospel, but I think it's a contradiction of the gospel. Not that God wants all His people to live in poverty, for He does give us "richly all things to enjoy" (1 Tim. 6:17). But in the light of Christ's birth, life, and death, and in the light of the sufferings and needs in our world today, how can the church justify supporting men and movements that waste its resources?

I think that some of our Christian celebrities have gotten into moral and financial problems because they started believing what people were saying about them. It must be difficult for a celebrity to come home to his family after a triumphant meeting or concert and be told to change the baby's diapers or to take out the garbage!

John was not a compromiser, a celebrity, or a *crowd pleaser*. A false prophet asks, "Is my message popular?" while the prophet of God asks, "Is my message true?" You can't please the crowd anyway, so why try? One day they want to play wedding, and the next day they want to play funeral! One week they complain because the preacher is in his study too much, and the next week they scold him for making too many visits! The preacher who caters to the crowd has forgotten the words of Thomas à Kempis, "The glory of good men is in their conscience and not in the mouths of men."[1] So much for media ratings.

Many ministries today are governed by popularity and not by integrity, by statistics and not by Scripture. Once the initial excitement was over, it's doubtful that John the Baptist's ministry could hold the interest of the modern religious media audience. For one thing, he got too personal; and he didn't care about his press coverage or his ratings. His only concern was this: "He [Christ] must increase, but I must decrease" (John 3:30).

The average Christian probably doesn't realize how important popularity is to ministry these days. When I became senior pastor at the Moody Church, publishers and conference directors began to pester me and "court" me, wanting me to write books for them and speak at their meetings. I wasn't fooled by all the attention. I knew that my name and my abilities were of secondary importance; the fact that I was at Moody Church was the most important thing. The Moody Church name would help to draw crowds and sell books.

A pastor phoned me and asked if I could come to his church to give a series of messages on worship. I couldn't accept his invitation because my schedule was full, but I gave him the name of a gifted friend who was leading exciting seminars on worship and could do a good job for him.

"I've never heard of him!" the pastor said.

"So what?" I replied. "Until this evening, I'd never heard of *you!* Are you looking for a celebrity or a speaker?"

My friend never got the invitation, and quite frankly, he didn't care. Somehow it seemed paradoxical that a pastor wanted somebody with a "big name" to teach his people how to worship God.

Our churches need preachers like Jeremiah and John the Baptist, servants of God who courageously stand for truth and who aren't intimidated by the crowd. We need the kind of preachers John Wesley described when he said:

> Give me one hundred preachers who fear nothing but sin and desire nothing but God, and I care not a straw

whether they be clergymen or laymen, such alone will shake the gates of hell and set up the Kingdom of God on earth.[2]

Our churches also need courageous leaders like Nehemiah who are willing to tackle the hard job of removing the rubbish, rebuilding the walls, and taking away the reproach of God's people. Preachers and leaders must work together if this integrity crisis is to be solved.

So, let's return to Nehemiah and consider him as our example of leadership integrity.

7
RECONSTRUCTION

Before we follow any man
we should look for the oil on his forehead.
We are under no spiritual obligation
to aid any man in any activity
that has not upon it the marks of the cross.

A.W. TOZER

Everything rises or falls with leadership, and this includes what we call "the work of the Lord." When we read the Bible, we meet men and women who were called to be leaders in hours of crisis. Some of them succeeded magnificently to the glory of God. Others failed miserably and only made the crisis worse.

History shows that a crisis has a way of producing at least three different kinds of leaders, and our present-day integrity crisis is no exception.

Usually the first kind of leader to emerge is the optimist who takes a painless, cosmetic approach to the situation. He deals only with surface blemishes and quickly convinces the public that things aren't so bad after all. "It's not that the problem is so serious," our leader says with a smile. "It's just that the news coverage is better. If we wait long enough, everything will work out, and the whole thing will soon be forgotten."

You'll recall that Jeremiah had to deal with leaders like that. "For they have healed the hurt of the daughter of My people slightly, / Saying, 'Peace, peace!' / When there is no peace" (8:11). Of course, some people want this kind of leader because he keeps them happy and demands no sacrifices from them. Machiavelli wrote in *The Prince*, "Men are so simple and so much inclined to obey immediate needs that a deceiver will never lack victims for his deceptions."[1]

The second kind of leader is more realistic: he admits that there are serious problems, and he promises to remedy the situation by getting busy. Give him the budget and the authority, and he'll set up new organizations, establish new goals, hire new people, and enforce new standards. While these short-term remedies are no doubt better than optimistic inertia, they are still only substitutes for the drastic changes that are really needed. Hiring a new crew and charting a new course won't keep the sinking ship afloat. The danger is that the passengers and crew may get so excited about the new equipment on board that they forget the ship needs to be rescued.

When the PTL scandal began to threaten public support of media ministries, one leader said, "The serious issue facing religious broadcasting is not what happened, but what should be done about it." He then suggested that the solution was a new organization to enforce higher standards of fiscal accountability. Nobody will deny that accountability is important, but it isn't the only answer. It's unwise to make a diagnosis and write a prescription without first carefully examining the patient. Personally, I have a greater fear of false gospels than I do of false audits.

The third kind of leader is the one we really need. He shuns the cosmetic approach, because he knows it's superficial, and the "quick fix" approach, because he knows it's temporary. He has the courage to face the problems honestly, the wisdom to understand them, the strength to do something about them, and the faith to trust God to do the rest. He isn't afraid of losing friends or making enemies. He can't be intimidated by threats or bought with bribes. He is God's man, and he isn't for sale.

Such a leader was Nehemiah, a man who shows us how to rebuild in a day of reproach.

Nehemiah was a displaced person, a Jew living in the palace of Artaxerxes I, king of Persia. As the king's cupbearer, he enjoyed prestige and wealth, authority and comfort. There was no reason why he should be concerned about his fellow Jews in Jerusalem, but he was. In fact, he cared enough to ask what things were like in the Holy City. To me, this is significant: he wanted to face facts honestly; he wasn't afraid of the truth.

One problem today is that many Christians don't really want to face facts. They live in a devotional dream world with eyes blind to the truth and ears open only to calm messages assuring them that all is well. The fact that some of the watchmen on the walls have gone to sleep not only doesn't disturb many church folks but it actually reassures them. No news always means good news.

But all is not well with the church, our speeches and statistics notwithstanding. We need a few more people like Nehemiah who care enough to inquire, even if the news they get isn't too encouraging: "The survivors who are left from the captivity in the province are there in great distress and reproach. The wall of Jerusalem is also broken down, and its gates are burned with fire" (Neh. 1:3).

Why should Nehemiah, the king's right-hand man, be concerned about the plight of fifty thousand Jews living over a thousand miles away? Suppose they *were* in distress and reproach? There were plenty of reasons (or excuses) to keep him uninvolved.

To begin with, what can one man do about such a difficult situation? Furthermore, was it *his* fault that the city had been destroyed a century and a half before then? No, his ancestors had sinned and brought God's judgment on Jerusalem. They were the ones who had rejected the messages of Jeremiah and the other prophets and had persisted in their idolatry. They were the ones who had sinned, not Nehemiah and his generation. How easy it would have been for Nehemiah to escape.

We saw this "escape" attitude expressed by too many Christians when the PTL scandal broke. The most popular pronouns used were *they* and *them,* in spite of the fact that Jesus taught us to use *we* and *us*. No, I'm not saying that all of us were to blame for what happened; but I am saying that we can't deny our oneness in the body of Christ and our responsibilities to one another. No matter how guilty others may have been, it seems heartless for us to stand aloof and point our fingers.

Nehemiah cared enough to inquire, and he also cared enough to identify. He sat down and wept!

Will Rogers was known for his laughter, but he also knew how to weep. One day he was entertaining at the Milton H. Berry Institute in Los Angeles, a hospital that specialized in rehabilitating polio victims and people with broken backs and other extreme physical handicaps. Of course, Rogers had everybody laughing, even patients in really bad condition; but then he suddenly left the platform and went to the rest room. Milton Berry followed him to give him a towel; and when he opened the door, he saw Will Rogers leaning against the wall, sobbing like a child. He closed the door, and in a few minutes, Rogers appeared back on the platform, as jovial as before.[2]

If you want to learn what a person is really like, ask three questions: What makes him laugh? What makes him angry? What makes him weep? These are fairly good tests of character that are especially appropriate for Christian leaders. I hear people saying, "We need angry leaders today!" or "The time has come to practice militant Christianity!" Perhaps, but "the wrath of man does not produce the righteousness of God" (James 1:20).

What we need today is not anger but *anguish,* the kind of anguish that Moses displayed when he broke the two tables of the law and then climbed the mountain to intercede for his people, or that Jesus displayed when He cleansed the temple and then wept over the city. *The difference between anger and anguish is a broken heart.* It's easy to get angry, especially at somebody else's sins; but it's not easy to look at sin, our own included, and weep over it.

Why did Nehemiah weep? Not because the city of his fathers was in ruins, but because the God of his fathers was being reproached by the enemy. Nehemiah's concern was for the glory of the Lord, not just for the welfare of the people. He mourned and wept; he fasted and prayed. His identification with the tragic situation in Jerusalem was so intense that the sorrow showed on his face, and the king saw it.

I wonder how many of us sit down and weep when we hear that a Christian leader has sinned or a ministry has fallen? I wonder how many of us mourn as we watch the news media have a heyday at the expense of the church? When somebody falls, many of us in places of leadership rush about to protect our own names and ministries, and we forget that it is God's name that must be magnified. Instead of identifying with the painful situation, we too often get as far away as we can.

Nehemiah identified not only with the shame and suffering, but also with the sins of his ancestors. "We have sinned against You," he told the Lord. "We have acted very corruptly against You" (Neh. 1:6–7). Note the pronoun: *we,* not *they.* While we certainly don't approve of what some of the PTL leaders have been accused of doing, neither do we endorse the self-righteous attitude that many believers displayed when they heard the sad news. Is any church or parachurch ministry spotless? And even if our ministries are clean to the glory of God, should we so harden our hearts that we can't even sit down and weep with those who weep?

Nehemiah cared enough to inquire, to identify, and to intercede. After he sat down and wept, he knelt down and prayed. We usually think of Nehemiah as a model executive, a man of action; but he was also a man of prayer. At least eleven incidents of prayer are recorded in his book. The leader who knows how to pray will know what God wants him to do.

Nehemiah 1:5–11 is the record of a truly great prayer in the Bible, the kind of prayer you can make your own because it touches your basic needs. Here you have intercession based on God's character ("O great and awesome God") and God's covenant ("You who keep Your covenant and mercy"). On the basis of God's character and covenant, Nehemiah confessed his sins and the sins of the people, and he claimed God's forgiveness.

If an evangelical scandal breaks again, I wonder what would happen if we media leaders would go to our knees *together* in prayer, not just for our own threatened ministries, but for all God's people? Could we not call a great concert of prayer and invite other ministries, pastors, and churches to join with us in confessing sin and seeking God's face? To be sure, many of us have prayed personally and are still praying; but perhaps there would have been a greater impact had we prayed and confessed our sins together.

Nehemiah's prayer was more than a prayer of confession; it was also a prayer of consecration as he made himself available to the Lord to do whatever needed to be done. *We are not really praying by faith unless we make ourselves available to be a part of the answer.* "Now to Him who is able to do exceedingly abundantly above all that we ask or think, according to the power *that works in us*" (Eph. 3:20, italics mine). It was not a matter of "Here am I—send my brother!" It was "Here am I, Lord, send me!"

This leads us to the final stage of Nehemiah's experience: he cared enough to get involved. He asked and inquired, sat down and wept, knelt down and prayed, and then got up and worked. He was a man with a broken heart, a man with believing prayers, a man with busy hands; and that's what it takes to rebuild in a day of reproach.

We sometimes forget that *Nehemiah paid a tremendous price to get involved.* He gave up the luxury and security of the palace for the ruins and dangers of Jerusalem. He sacrificed honor and ease for ridicule and toil. In fifty-two days, he removed the rubbish, rebuilt the walls, and restored the gates of Jerusalem, tasks that the enemy said couldn't be done. Alexander Whyte perfectly described the Nehemiah type of leader: "He will not begin till he has counted the cost. And then he will not stop till he has finished his work."[3] And we might add that he does it all to the glory of God.

The most impressive thing about Nehemiah is his integrity: he had a single eye in his dedication to the task and a single heart in his devotion to the Lord. A hard-working man, he was definitely not a celebrity trying to build a kingdom for himself. When ridiculed, he prayed. When threatened, he prayed and took a sword in one hand and a tool in the other and kept on working. When invited to compromise, he replied, "I am doing a great work, so that I cannot come down" (Neh. 6:3). He saw the greatness of his God and the greatness of the work, and he refused to budge.

Nehemiah was especially careful about finances. When the people started to exploit one another, he rebuked them and reminded them of his own disciplined lifestyle (see Neh. 5). As governor, Nehemiah could have enjoyed many financial privileges; but he willingly set them aside for the good of the work. He paid his own bills and then generously shared what he had with 150 guests who sat at his table. "I did not demand the governor's provisions," he wrote, "because the bondage was heavy on this people" (5:18).

While Nehemiah was governor of Jerusalem, some outside merchants set up their wares and did a profitable business on the Sabbath day (see 13:15–22). Alas, some Jews were also involved. The governor could have joined the enterprise and made more money. Instead, he put a stop to it and made more enemies. It's good to have a leader who knows the difference between prices and values and whose conscience isn't for sale.

He knew how to handle both the responsibilities and the privileges of his office: the responsibilities didn't break his spirit, and the privileges didn't build his ego. Like all good leaders, he carried more than his share of the burden and took less than his share of the credit. To him, the work was not a job, it was a ministry; and for that reason, he expected to make sacrifices. "Privilege never confers security," said John Henry Jowett. "It rather provides the conditions of the fiercest strife."[4]

Nehemiah knew how to work with people and how to get people to work for the Lord. Every true leader begets leaders. He doesn't use others to build his authority; he uses his authority to build others. Nehemiah (the younger man) had no problem serving with Ezra (the older man): the administrator and the scribe were as one because both were dedicated to the great work of the Lord.

When we consider that the work was accomplished in fifty-two days and that the workers, both men and women, were not trained builders, we have to give the glory to God. But bringing glory to God's name is what ministry is all about. If Nehemiah had adopted the approach of some contemporary religious organizations, he would have spent the first several months "building an image" so that the public would know him and respond to his leadership. Public relations firms tell us that they can make a nobody into a somebody in a short time, given enough budget and media cooperation. Fortunately, Nehemiah didn't take that approach.

What did this man and his associates accomplish by the grace of God? They accomplished three difficult tasks that, spiritually speaking, the church needs to accomplish today.

First, they rebuilt the walls. We today who live in modern cities and suburbs may not appreciate how important walls were to the people of Nehemiah's day. A walled city was a city of distinction and a city with defenses against the enemy. Walls stood for both separation and safety. One of the most important things a ruler did in that day was to strengthen and extend the city walls, and the first thing an enemy tried to do was to break the walls down. No wonder David prayed, "Build the walls of Jerusalem" (Ps. 51:18). Charles H. Spurgeon said:

> The New Jerusalem must, in like manner, be sur-
> rounded and preserved by a broad wall of nonconformity
> to the world, and *separation* from its customs and spirit.
> The tendency of these days is to break down the holy bar-
> rier, and make the distinction between the church and
> the world purely nominal.[5]

What some people call "separation from the world" is really isolation from the world, and what others call "penetration into the world" may be nothing more than old-fashioned compromise masquerading under a new name. When the church, trying to reach the world, became like the world, she lost her impact on the world. How tragic that we cooperated with the enemy in *breaking down our own walls!* We lost our own distinctiveness and destroyed our own defenses.

The fact that some believers have practiced an extreme form of separation is no excuse for us to throw the baby out with the bath water. "We are not to be isolated but insulated," said Vance Havner, "moving in the midst of evil but untouched by it."[6] Separation is contact without contamination. Jesus was "holy, harmless, undefiled, separate from sinners" (Heb. 7:26), yet He was "a friend of tax collectors and sinners" (Luke 7:34).

In our desire to escape "legalism," I fear we have embraced a subtle form of antinomianism (the idea that salvation by grace negates our obligation to moral law), with results that would have driven our fathers to their knees in prayer: treating the marriage covenant lightly, adopting the lifestyle of "the rich and famous," using the world's approach in merchandising the gospel, ignoring the Lord's Day, refusing to enforce standards, and even watering down our preaching so people won't be offended.

G. K. Chesterton advised, "Don't ever take a fence down

until you know the reason why it was put up."[7] Fences and walls not only keep things out; they also *keep things in.* The church always loses its valuables, including valuable people, to the world when the walls of separation are torn down.

In addition to rebuilding the walls, Nehemiah and his workers restored the gates. The city gate in an Eastern city was much more than a place of entrance and exit; it was also a place of authority where the city officials met to transact business. When Jesus wanted to illustrate the authority and victory of His church, He said that "the gates of Hades shall not prevail against it" (Matt. 16:18).

It's possible to have gates without walls, but the gates won't do what gates are supposed to do. During World War II, the iron fence around a London park was removed to help the war effort; but the ornamental gates remained. Each evening, the guard dutifully locked the gates to keep people out! We smile at this, but I wonder if the church today isn't doing the same thing.

The strongest walls are useless if the gates are weak or if the gatekeepers are careless or disloyal. The Great Wall of China was penetrated by enemies at least three times, and each time the guards were bribed. The church desperately needs strong gates and loyal gatekeepers.

This is a good place to say something about the importance of dedicated board members. After all, in our various ministries, the board helps to guard the gates and make sure the ministry is secure theologically, organizationally, and financially. More than one ministry has been ruined because the official board didn't do its job.

It's not important that board members be rich or famous, but it is important that they be honest and faithful. They are God's chosen gatekeepers, and they must be alert and courageous. When board members are intimidated by the leaders of the organization or influenced by the donors, it doesn't take long for a ministry to start to fall apart. I once resigned from a mission board (now defunct) because the founder changed the constitution so he could run things his way. I lost a friend, but at least I saved my conscience.

Of course, during this project Nehemiah and his workers had to remove the rubbish that hindered them from building the wall. They didn't have to lay a new foundation. All they had to do was clear away the rubbish, expose the old foundation, and build on it. But that wasn't easy. "The strength of the laborers is failing," the men of Judah complained, "and there is so much rubbish that we are not able to build the wall" (Neh. 4:10).

The importance of the foundation can't be emphasized enough: it determines the size of the structure, the shape, and the strength. To build the wall on no foundation, or on the wrong foundation, would be both foolish and dangerous. To find the original foundation, Nehemiah's workmen had to first get rid of the rubbish.

It is easy for us to accumulate trash and then get so accustomed to it that we think it's treasure! Mother cleans out the basement while father is at work; but as soon as he arrives home, he moves "selected junk" back into the basement. In spite of flea markets and garage sales, we end up with more stuff than we started with.

Wise is the leader who knows rubbish when he sees it and who has the courage to cart it away. Like Israel at Passover, every ministry needs a regular housecleaning that will leave it purer and better. Perhaps we've collected organizational rubbish that's getting in the way of progress. Or it may be doctrinal rubbish that's grieving the Holy Spirit and hindering

His power. Maybe the whole ministry needs trimming because we have too many people, too many committees, too many activities, and we can't find the foundation. Carting away the rubbish isn't a popular job or an easy one; but it's an important job.

Yes, everything rises or falls with leadership, simply because followers eventually become like their leaders. One generation of power-hungry leaders can cripple the church for years to come. We know what we need: preachers like Jeremiah and John the Baptist and leaders like Nehemiah.

But we need something else: intercessors like Moses. If we don't get back to prayer, there is no hope for revival in the church.

8
REPRIEVE

---

*God never gives us discernment
in order that we may criticize,
but that we may intercede.*

OSWALD CHAMBERS

Even if all our preachers were like Jeremiah and all our leaders like Nehemiah, we would still not solve the problems created by the integrity crisis. Why? Because behind the preachers and the leaders must be the intercessors who lay hold of God and claim His blessings for His church. *One of the greatest needs in the church today is for intercessory prayer.* We need intercessors like Moses.

While preparing a series of radio messages, I was surprised to discover that the Bible records at least twenty-five instances of prayer in the life of Moses. We usually think of Moses as a liberator or a legislator, but we forget that he was also a great prayer warrior. In fact, Moses is a good example of what it means for us to intercede on behalf of those who have sinned. We can find the record in Exodus 32-33.

Moses had been alone with God on Mount Sinai, receiving the law that he would deliver to the people. But he stayed away too long, and Israel became restless, like sheep without a shepherd. God's people had (and still have) a difficult time waiting and walking by faith. They asked Aaron to do something, so he made a golden calf to represent God; and with great joy, the people declared a holiday. At last, something exciting was happening! There was something they could see and do!

Of course, God saw it all and called it to the attention of His servant Moses: "Go, get down! For your people whom you brought out of the land of Egypt have corrupted themselves" (Exod. 32:7). It looked like the end of the nation, but Moses prayed and God turned away His wrath.

When Moses arrived in the camp, he saw the people engaged in a religious orgy as they danced around the golden calf and supposedly worshiped Jehovah God. In hot and holy anger, Moses broke the two tables of stone, destroyed the calf, and judged the people. Then he climbed Mt. Sinai and once again interceded for his people. The upshot was that God punished the offenders, spared the nation, and agreed to go with Israel as they journeyed, all because Moses prayed.

Let's find out what this event means to the church today.

To intercede means "to plead with somebody on behalf of another person." In the Christian vocabulary, it means to plead with God on behalf of His children who have needs. We are never more like the Lord Jesus Christ than when we are interceding for others, because that's what He's doing in heaven today (see Heb. 7:24–25).

The church has always needed intercessors because God runs His work on prayer. "If the veil of the world's machinery were lifted off," said McCheyne, "how much we would find is done in answer to the prayers of God's children."[1] God makes it clear that we accomplish nothing eternal apart from prayer, no matter how successful we may appear to be. God help the ministry that can get along without believing prayer! "Whether we like it or not," said Spurgeon, "asking is the rule of the kingdom."[2]

Prayer is vital, not only because God has commanded it, but also because He has ordained that through it His people grow in faith and dependence so that He alone gets the glory. True servants of God depend on prayer and aren't embarrassed to admit it; but celebrities merely talk about prayer to impress their followers. Prayer isn't the power of a celebrity's ministry; it's merely a small part of his or her religious equipment.

One reason I went into Youth for Christ back in 1957 was because I was challenged by the organization's dependence on prayer. I was stirred by the sight of well-known pastors and businessmen on their knees, seeking the blessing of God; and I was especially moved by the all-night prayer meetings at the annual Winona Lake YFC Convention. The late Peter Deyneka, Sr., who conducted the meetings, often reminded us, "Much prayer, much power! No prayer, no power!" Moses would have agreed with Peter.

Why do we need intercessors? Because too many of God's people today are doing what Israel did in Moses' day: worshiping a golden calf. A *golden* calf, mind you, not one made of wood or stone. They were worshiping the great god Mammon.

They made a calf in Horeb,
And worshiped the molded image.
Thus they changed their glory
Into the image of an ox that eats grass.

They forgot God their Savior,
Who had done great things in Egypt (Ps. 106:19–21).

Most of us are so accustomed to having wealth that we're offended if anybody accuses us of worshiping money. Compared to Christians in other parts of the world, we are wealthy indeed; and in subtle ways we dance around the golden calf and sing our songs of praise. Money is too often our measure of ministry. Like Israel at Sinai, we claim to be worshiping the true God; but our image of that God is—gold.

For example, we boast about our budgets. Peter confessed openly, "Silver and gold I do not have" (Acts 3:6); and Paul wrote, "As poor, yet making many rich" (2 Cor. 6:10). If the average pastor talked like that today, his members would probably blush with shame. A big budget is a sign that God is blessing!

After preaching at an influential church that was searching for a new pastor, I was told by one of the officers, "If you were our pastor, you would never have any financial worries." I assured him that my wife and I didn't fret about those things because the Lord had always taken good care of us. I had a suspicion that Mammon was quietly controlling some of the leaders, whether the people knew it or not.

We also boast about our buildings. It's disturbing how many church bulletins and letterheads carry pictures of buildings, as if brick and mortar were the most important parts of ministry. It's unfortunate that church boards often have an easier time finding money for building maintenance and expansion than they do for ministry and missions. When he spoke at the dedication of the new Houses of Parliament, Winston Churchill said, "First we make our buildings and then our buildings make us." How true!

There isn't a thing wrong with budgets or buildings per se.

It's scriptural to pay the pastor a sensible salary, since the laborer is worthy of his hire (see Luke 10:7); and it's practical to have a "church house" where the family can meet for worship and service. But when these things become the measure of ministry and the most important mark of spiritual blessing, we've built a golden calf. We've exchanged God's transcendent glory for the temporary glory that money can buy.

It's also disturbing to see that ministry is now for sale the way any other service is for sale. If you want certain "Christian music artists," you sign a contract and agree to pay a fixed fee, which is usually high. I haven't met any preachers who follow this policy, but I suspect there are some. I doubt that the apostles or prophets ever charged a fee.

We need intercessors today because our values are confused. We think we're rich and in need of nothing, but really we are "wretched, miserable, poor, blind, and naked" (Rev. 3:17). We agree with Jesus that it's impossible to serve *both* God and Mammon (see Matt. 6:24), and we don't even try. Rather, *we worship Mammon in the place of God and thank God for giving it to us!* The extravagant lifestyle of some religious media people, repugnant as it may be, is duplicated on a smaller scale in many homes and churches. We're so used to it that we don't even notice it.

The people of Israel sacrificed so that they could enjoy their golden calf. They donated their wealth, and they even got up early in the morning to eat and drink and play (see Exod. 32:6). I've met church people who complain about missionary offerings ("Are they begging again?") but never think twice about spending thousands of dollars to enjoy a "Christian vacation" or purchase another unnecessary "adult toy." People who would find it difficult to get up early for a prayer meeting have no problem getting up early for a time of "fun." Individuals sacrifice for the things they really love.

Just as the idolatry and immorality of the golden calf event disgust us, so does the compromise of Aaron. He tried to alibi his way out of it, but Moses knew that his brother, God's high priest, was guilty. Aaron represents those religious leaders who give the people what they want instead of what they need, who are more concerned about pleasing people than about pleasing God. Aaron's cooperation with the carnal crowd probably made him the most popular man in camp (see Exod. 32:1–6).

So much for the need for intercessors. Now let's look at Moses as an example of the kind of intercessors we need.

To begin with, we need an intercessor who will spend time alone with God, listening to His Word and beholding His glory, just as Moses did. An intercessor can't be in a hurry; the place of intercession isn't a fast-food shop. The church today sings "Take time to be holy," but how many of us really practice what we sing? Instead of taking time to be holy, we use daily devotional guides that require us to spend only a few minutes each day in "spiritual exercise." We read a Bible verse and some digested "spiritual thoughts," and perhaps a poem and a prayer, and then we go on our way rejoicing because we have spent time with the Lord.

I used to think that this kind of devotional life was better than none at all, but I've changed my mind. Anything that is a substitute for God's Word is bound to be harmful to spiritual growth. I'm not suggesting that using devotional guides is wrong; I have a large collection of them in my library, and I use them. I've even written a few myself. But devotional guides must be *supplements to God's Word, not substitutes for God's Word*. I reach for a devotional book *after* I've spent time in the Word and in prayer, in personal fellowship with the Lord.

"I have so much to do," said John Wesley, "that I must

spend several hours in prayer before I am able to do it."³ No wonder he turned Great Britain upside down: he knew how to intercede.

Like Moses, an intercessor must expect to be misunderstood and criticized. After all, you can't be a popular person if you let your priorities keep you away from the committee meetings, seminars, and conferences that everybody else attends. It's difficult to understand how some of today's preachers get time to prepare themselves and their messages when they are constantly running to some "evangelical watering hole" to bless the saints. Maybe they don't prepare their own messages or write their own books. Maybe they're content to be like bad photographs: overexposed and underdeveloped.

A true intercessor must be unselfish. God offered to destroy Israel and build a new nation through Moses, and Moses refused the offer (see Exod. 32:10). God made the same offer when Israel rebelled at Kadesh Barnea, and again Moses said no (see Num. 14:12). His desire was not for personal promotion; his desire was for the good of the people and for the glory of God.

All selfishness is bad, but it is especially bad when it invades the prayer closet. "You ask and do not receive, because you ask amiss, that you may spend it on your pleasures" (James 4:3). What a contrast to our Lord's Gethsemane prayer: "Father, if it is Your will, take this cup away from Me; nevertheless not My will, but Yours, be done" (Luke 22:42). Selfish prayers are dangerous because God might give us what we ask!

An effective intercessor prays on the basis of God's character and God's covenant. (You'll recall that Nehemiah also prayed that way.) Moses reminded the Lord of His covenant promises to Abraham, Isaac, and Jacob, and he pointed out that *God's glory* was at stake, not the glory of the nation. If Israel didn't make it to Canaan, all the other nations would say, "Their God can start things, but He can't finish them!"

I'm convinced that some of us in evangelical ministry have escaped the wrath of God only because He didn't want to give the enemy more ammunition for opposing the gospel. Whether deliberately or ignorantly, we've worshiped the golden calf, or helped others to worship it; and God's been patient with us. However, in this recent crisis, God may be saying to us what He said to David, "By this deed you have given great occasion to the enemies of the LORD to blaspheme" (2 Sam. 12:14). I won't go into detail. You've followed the radio and TV talk shows, read the columnists, and seen the comic strips, and no doubt you have hung your head in shame. I have.

An effective intercessor faces facts honestly and isn't soft on sin. Moses rebuked Aaron and the people and humbled them before the Lord. He even endorsed the killing of three thousand idolaters; something we would not do today; but we could use that kind of spirit of obedience to God and hatred of sin. Then he went back up to the mountain to plead with God and to offer to die in Israel's place. "Yet now, if You will forgive their sin—but if not, I pray, blot me out of Your book which You have written" (Exod. 32:32). An intercessor knows the seriousness of sin and is willing to pay the price to help others and to glorify God.

The thing that kept Moses going was his vision of the glory of God. "Please," he asked God on the mount, "show me Your glory" (Exod. 33:18). The scene in the valley was depressing, but the glorious revelation on the mountaintop was exciting. Moses saw the glory of God! That vision didn't minimize Israel's sins (if anything, it made them look more hideous), but it did vitalize Moses' faith and enable him to go back into the valley and take command again.

One dismal day during this recent crisis, I started to feel discouraged. I'd read the news stories and chatted over the phone with some of my media friends, when the enemy started to whisper, "It really isn't worth it, is it? All these years, you and Back to the Bible have kept your hands clean and tried to honor the Lord; and the public doesn't seem to know the difference. They're putting all you media ministries into one basket and tossing that basket on the city dump! It isn't worth it, is it?"

Believe me, it was a dark hour in my soul. I couldn't find any way back into the light until I centered my thoughts and prayers on the glory of God. When I realized that God's glory was far more important than *anybody*'s reputation, budget, or ministry, the light began to dawn, and the burden began to lift. The Lord reminded me of a verse He gave me one night in an intensive care ward where I was hovering between life and death: "Great is the LORD, and greatly to be praised; / And His greatness is unsearchable" (Ps. 145:3).

I don't understand all the ways of the Lord, but I believe that ultimately, in some way, this crisis is going to bring glory to God. Meanwhile, we have to live with the shame and faithfully stay at our posts serving the Lord.

And we must take time to be holy—and to intercede.

9
REALITY

Television is the supremely powerful drug.
I end up living my existence
before the very thing that eliminates me.

JACQUES ELLUL

During this integrity crisis, the focus of attention has been
on morals, money, and message, in that order; but not much
has been said about the *medium* involved, namely, television. I
may be wrong, but I think that the medium of television
helped to create the scandal. Had the people involved been in
any other medium, some things might have been different.
I'm not excusing; I'm explaining. We must understand the
part that television played in producing the integrity crisis, *because television continues to exert that same kind of influence on the church
today*.

Let me begin with a few media memories.

I was privileged to grow up during the great days of radio,
when people planned schedules around listening to "The
Lone Ranger," "Jack Armstrong," "Lum and Abner," and

"Jack Benny." I also remember the early years of Christian radio and the programs we heard from WMBI in Chicago. Those were the days of my middle-namesake, Wendell P. Loveless, as well as Ralph Stewart, Robert Parsons, George Beverly Shea, and a host of other gifted people whose ministries God greatly blessed. In those days, radio was a vital part of our lives. It brought us music and the spoken word from everywhere in the world.

When Christian movies burst on the scene, we got excited. We'd seen "missionary pictures," but this type of film was new. Some of the early films were nothing but object lessons or action sermons put on film or perhaps a sermon delivered by a great preacher. Harry Ironside's *Charge That to My Account* comes to mind. A battle waged in the Christian press as to whether God could bless Christian films since the people in them were acting a part. A. W. Tozer opposed Christian films with a passion, but they went right on. Now Christian films are an accepted part of church life.

Along came television with a new cast of characters, like Howdy Doody, Kukla, Fran, and Ollie, Captain Video, and Ed Sullivan, plus the reruns of old movies our Sunday school teachers had warned us not to see in the theaters. Many radio stars moved into TV only to discover that television was not "radio plus pictures." It was an entirely new kind of medium with a power all its own, a power that had to be obeyed or the program wouldn't succeed. The media analyst, Marshall McLuhan, tried to explain the new phenomenon to us in his books, particularly *Understanding Media: The Extensions of Man;* but it was easier to watch TV than read books about TV. Not everybody agreed with McLuhan, but nobody could safely ignore him. After all these years, he has pretty much convinced us that the medium is the message.

The first religious television program I recall seeing was

Percy Crawford's "Youth on the March." It was an adaptation of his popular Sunday afternoon radio broadcast, "The Young People's Church of the Air." I also remember watching Charles Fuller when "The Old Fashioned Revival Hour" tried television for about six months in 1950 and then gave it up. Of all the TV preachers of that era, perhaps Fulton J. Sheen best understood how to use the new medium. I didn't agree with all of his theology, but he certainly knew how to get the message across. With his sacred robes, his dramatic delivery, his blackboard, and his piece of chalk, he seemed to understand how TV worked.

Those were peaceful days when we dreamed of great things to come. The air waves weren't cluttered with preachers competing for our time and money, and many Christian people were convinced that the media were God's gifts to the church to reach the world with the gospel. If we just had enough time and money, we could get the job done. A media millennium was around the corner.

Now, over forty years later, as I reflect on these things, I've drawn some gut-level conclusions that are strictly personal and without statistical defense. Here they are.

Christian radio has made a significant contribution both to local churches and to world missions and should continue to do so. As for films, they've been a useful tool; but my guess is they will be replaced by video. When it comes to religious TV, I think we evangelicals missed the boat completely *because we didn't take time to understand the medium and how it worked*. Like the unsuccessful comedians who tried to duplicate radio on TV, we've tried to put "church" on TV, but we haven't had great success.

Now we have discovered two facts about television that for some reason eluded us for years. The first is that television is an *entertainment* medium, so that whatever it communicates is

96

transformed into entertainment. The second is that television is a *commercial* industry, and the name of the game is money. Even the well-known television executive, Fred Friendly, has admitted this. He said, "Because television can make so much money doing its worst, it often cannot afford to do its best."[1]

You may wonder where this discussion is leading, but please stay with me. We didn't think about these things years ago, and now we're in trouble. We can't change the past, but we might be able to do something about the future.

By its very nature, television is an entertainment medium. This doesn't mean we can't learn anything by watching it, because we can. (Some people learn things they shouldn't learn.) However, whatever we learn from television, we learn primarily from *seeing* and not from *hearing*. This distinction is important, because the emphasis in the Bible is on *hearing* and not on *seeing*. "So then faith comes by hearing, and hearing by the word of God" (Rom. 10:17). Television has helped to create a society of watchers, not listeners, people who are fascinated by pictures, not educated by words.

The first step toward man's fall was taken when Eve substituted *what she saw* (the tree was "pleasant to the sight," Gen. 2:9) for *what she heard from God* ("you shall not eat" from it, Gen. 2:17). After the Fall, Adam and Eve ran and hid when they heard the voice of God. Instead of communicating, the Word was *ex*communicating; but the fault was man's, not God's. Since that time, God has graciously and clearly been speaking to sinful men and women, trying to bridge that tragic communications gap; but most people don't want to hear.[2]

When the Son of God was on earth, His most important ministry was proclaiming the Word of God, not performing miracles. "If anyone has ears to hear, let him hear!" (Mark

7:16). To be sure, His miracles were important as evidence of His messiahship and proof of His great compassion for the needy; but declaring the Word had first priority. Unfortunately, the crowds wanted to *see;* they didn't want to *hear*. One of the major themes in John's gospel is the conflict between faith and sight. Crowds of people "believed" in Jesus only because they saw His miracles; but Jesus didn't believe in them (see John 2:23–25). He encouraged *hearing* and not *seeing*.

It's significant that God's greatest prophet, John the Baptist, came as a "voice" and not as a miracle worker (see John 1:23; 10:40–42). His emphasis was on preaching the Word of God. In presenting Jesus Christ to the nation, John gave the people something to hear so they would understand what they were seeing: "Behold! The Lamb of God who takes away the sin of the world!" (John 1:29). God has ordained that what we see is understood by what we hear. "The connection between Word and Truth is of such a nature," says philosopher Jacques Ellul, "that nothing can be known of truth apart from language."[3]

For the most part, television divorces hearing from seeing and creates a seductive, unreal world that appears very real. Ellul calls it "substitute reality."[4] If you turned off the picture and listened to the sound, you would never know what was really going on. This would not be true of programs that focus primarily on listening to words, such as "Meet the Press" or "Firing Line" *or the average religious TV program*. Except for watching the preacher's features and gestures, and seeing him hold up his latest book, you'd lose nothing of the essential content of the average religious TV program if you sat there blindfolded. In fact, being blindfolded and removing the distractions might improve your enjoyment of the program!

Now we've come to the heart of the matter. If the most important work of the church is the preaching of the Word, and the greatest need of the lost world is the hearing of the Word,

why should we glorify a medium like television that empha-
sizes *seeing* rather than *hearing?* What does TV add to our ministry? I say it adds nothing to our ministry, *but it can take a great
deal away*. TV puts God's people and God's Word into a context that can rob the message of reality.

Communications theorist Neil Postman explains that it is
"not that television is entertaining but that it has made entertainment itself the natural format for the representation of all
experience."[5] Whatever we watch on television, including a religious service, we watch in an entertainment context. No
matter what the program is, even a devastating documentary,
we don't take it too seriously. Why? Because the world of television is not "real."

Malcolm Muggeridge, former director of the BBC (British
Broadcasting Company), claims that "this medium, *by its nature,* doesn't lend itself to constructive purposes."[6] Educators
are discovering that video isn't the magic teaching tool they
once thought it was. Postman says, "We now know that 'Sesame Street' encourages children to love school only if school is
like 'Sesame Street.'"[7]

Now we can begin to understand why television is a threat
to Christian ministry: ministry isn't supposed to be entertainment, and a preacher isn't supposed to be a performer.
True ministry implies involvement: we're worshiping in the
holy presence of God, and we're obligated to hear God's Word
and obey it. When we put religion on TV, a subtle force goes
to work that transforms everything. *The viewer does not attend the
same service as the people in the sanctuary or in the TV studio*. The
people in the congregation can be participants; the viewer at
home is a spectator. The congregation is a living corporate fellowship, assembled for worship; the viewer is a solitary
watcher, even if he's not alone. Religion on TV is not the same
as religion in person. It's a new kind of religion altogether.

But that isn't all. As I was preparing this chapter, the latest issue of *the reid report* arrived on my desk, and I was happy to discover that my longtime friend Russ Reid agrees with me. In his lead article ("The Bakker Affair—What Can It Teach Us?"), Russ explains concisely why television is not the best medium for our kind of Christian ministry.

I believe many of the people involved in the electronic church are honest and are doing their work out of a deep sense of commitment. But I also believe they are wrong on four counts.

1. *The electronic church is a bad use of media.* As a whole, the mass media is not a very efficient means of bringing people to a decision about church, or any other kind of personal commitment. . . .

2. *The electronic church is a distortion of the church.* The message of the electronic church is extremely seductive. Its people are prettier. Its programs more potent. Its possibilities more persuasive. It seems to be saying, "I'll show you an easier way, where everything is music, dance and miracles. . . ."

3. *The electronic church is advertising that misleads.* Because of the nature of the medium, the electronic preacher is forced to reduce the message to a slogan, an oversimplification of truth that promises too much and delivers too little. . . .

4. *The electronic church is bad evangelism.* Television preachers justify their fund raising on the basis that they are reaching the unchurched. Yet the facts do not support their claim. In a study done for the National Council of Churches and the National Religious Broadcasters in 1984, it was estimated that 13 million people watch television preachers at least once during the week. Of the audience, only one million were unchurched. Yet the electronic church is spending at least *one billion dollars* to reach that million unchurched people.[8]

Another factor is the dangerous tendency of television to manufacture celebrities. "Television's strongest point," claims Postman, "is that it brings personalities into our hearts, not abstractions into our heads."[9] What develops is a "fan club mentality" in people so loyal to the cause that they won't even face the truth about their idols.

The television preacher who wants to can build himself a kingdom at the expense of others: the integrity of the board and the honesty and generosity of the followers. Human nature craves its heroes and thrives on vicarious success. The apostles fought this sin from the beginning. When Cornelius fell at Peter's feet, the apostle said, "Stand up; I myself am also a man" (Acts 10:26). Paul and Barnabus refused to be treated like gods (see Acts 14:8–18). When King Herod accepted the worship of men, God killed him (see Acts 12:20–23).

The Bible doesn't encourage the celebrity approach. "We find that Scripture is sparing in the information that it gives on people while it is lavish in what it tells us about God," writes Eugene Peterson. "It refuses to feed our lust for hero worship. It will not pander to our adolescent desire to join a fan club. The reason is, I think, clear enough. Fan clubs encourage secondhand living."[10]

When you combine the secondhand living of the fan club with the unreality of television, you end up with a brand of Christianity that's frightening to behold; *and yet it is the only "religion" some people profess!* They're living on substitutes and don't know it. If they were confronted with the genuine article, they wouldn't recognize it or be willing to pay the price to get it.

"But haven't people been saved through television ministries?" somebody may ask. Perhaps some have, but the end doesn't justify the means. "I would not favor a fiction to keep

101

the whole world out of hell," wrote George MacDonald. "The hell that a lie would keep any man out of is doubtless the very best place for him to go. It is truth . . . that saves the world."[11]

When people ask me why I'm not ministering on television, I usually smile and reply, "Because I have a perfect face for radio." But I've just explained the real reason: I don't think television and Bible ministry really go together. I'm not saying that you can't teach the truth over television, or preach it, or sing it, because you can. Some fine people are seeking to minister over television these days—some of them my friends—and I pray for them. However, I wonder if they wouldn't see more fruit if that same amount of money were put into other kinds of ministry.

The NCC/NRB survey that Russ Reid mentioned uncovered some interesting facts about the world of religious television. For one thing, it's not as big as some people want us to think. TV preachers who claim to have ten or twenty million viewers are whistling in the dark.

Religious TV does a good job of reinforcing what people already believe, but it fails when it comes to changing or deepening beliefs. Most of the people who regularly watch religious programs are already church members, or at least church attenders, with almost half attending at least one service a week. Only 6 percent of all viewers send regular contributions to television preachers, with an average of about thirty-five dollars per contribution. Only 7 percent said that watching religious TV increased their church involvement, while 3 percent said it made their involvement decrease.

The researchers concluded that most people watched religious television programs for two main reasons: (1) to strengthen and support what they already believed, and (2) to protest against the evil things presented on commercial television (homosexuality, abortion, pornography, etc.). In the areas of worship, evangelism, and education, religious TV is not a success.

There's one area, however where religious TV appears to be a success: the manufacturing of religious celebrities. No other medium offers greater opportunities to the religious huckster whose main concern is something other than ministry. "Show business" Christianity will always have its followers.

Mike Yaconelli said it eloquently in his "Back Door" column in *The Wittenberg Door:*

> The church has been mesmerized by power. We stand in awe of the beauty queen, the pro-football player, the wealthy businessman, and we willingly pay millions of dollars to anyone who will take our money and prove to us that we are the majority; that we are respectable; that we are the winners. We gladly allow these personages of power to travel in their private jets with their loyal platoon of executive assistants and press secretaries. We gladly give our substance to vicariously share with them as they wine and dine with presidents, scurry from one TV studio to the next, and whisk in and out of airports in long, black limousines. These power personalities have become our evangelical gigolos. We gladly prostitute our money, our time, and all that we have, so that we can flaunt them in front of those who do not believe that we are, in fact, winners. And it isn't their fault. It's ours.[12]

I rest my case.

10
RICHES

That man is admired above all men,
who is not influenced by money.

CICERO

"God and Money!" shouted the cover of *Time*'s August 3, 1987, issue. Beginning on page 48, *Time* announced what the public had long suspected: not everybody who says "Lord, Lord" can be trusted to get money honestly or handle it wisely. People lost no time responding to the news, and soon many religious organizations saw a dramatic decrease in contributions. Even ministries that had impeccable reputations suffered from the fallout. The public had lost confidence: it was an integrity crisis.

This wasn't the first time a religious empire had fallen, nor will it be the last. But it may well have been the first time a collapse involved so much money and so many people and got so much attention from the press for so long a time. Money and morals will always interest the public, so the press took advantage of it. You can't blame them; they have to make money, too.

I was told in seminary that pride, money, and sex are the enemy's chief weapons for ruining a ministry, and often they work together. A religious leader gets wealthy and famous, and then proud, and then he becomes a law unto himself and does what he pleases. After all, can't God's successful servants live above His law? In view of the fact that our Lord was humble, poor, and pure, you would expect His disciples to follow His example; but that isn't always the case.

The sequence is familiar. First a man or a woman feels called to ministry and sincerely wants to serve. But ministry takes money. Even Jesus had friends who helped Him pay His bills (see Luke 8:3), and Paul accepted support from both churches (see Phil. 4:15-16) and individuals (2 Tim. 1:15-18). Ministry takes money, but we have to be careful that *money doesn't start taking the ministry*. When that happens, ministry stops, and the organization turns into a religious business. Money becomes an end in itself and not a means to an end.

Television is an expensive medium, so we shouldn't be surprised if TV preachers get worried about money, especially if they enjoy an extravagant lifestyle that somebody has to support. But even the most modest TV preachers have to meet big budgets as they genuinely seek to serve the Lord; and it takes money. How they get that money and what they do with it depends on their integrity.

There are at least three myths about money and religion that we need to bury. The first is that money is neither good nor bad; it's neutral, and it all depends on how it's used. If this is true, why did Jesus call riches "unrighteous mammon" (Luke 16:9)? And why did He warn about "the deceitfulness of riches" (Matt. 13:22)? He seems to be saying that wealth is defiling and deceitful *of itself,* and that only God can sanctify it for noble uses.

I agree with Richard Foster: "Behind money are invisible spiritual powers, powers that are seductive and deceptive, powers that demand an all-embracing devotion."[1] Wealth is dangerous, and even the most devoted Christian can be trapped into worshiping Mammon *and not even realize he's doing it.*

Mammon is the Aramaic word for wealth of all kinds. It comes from a root meaning "that in which one trusts" or "that which is entrusted." This suggests that wealth is something entrusted to us by God, something God doesn't want us to trust. He wants us to trust Him. When the Jews used the word, it was almost always in a negative sense; and that's the way Jesus used it. He said, "No one can serve two masters; for either he will hate the one and love the other, or else he will be loyal to the one and despise the other. You cannot serve God and mammon" (Matt. 6:24).

Mammon is wealth personified, and Jesus has warned us not to relate to Mammon the way we relate to God. We must not try to put them on the same level in our lives. Money can control our attention and affection if we aren't careful. Foster points out that "money has many of the characteristics of deity. It gives security, can induce guilt, gives us freedom, gives us power and seems omnipresent. Most sinister of all, however, is its bid for omnipotence."[2]

Money wants to claim the loyalty and love that belong only to God, and it has the power to capture us if we're not careful. Money is a marvelous servant but a terrible master, and only a disciplined devotion to God can enable us to keep Mammon in its rightful place. In today's world, success is measured by money and possessions; and it's easy for Christians to endorse these false standards if we're not wary. Jesus said, "Take heed and beware of covetousness, for one's life does not consist in the abundance of the things he possesses" (Luke 12:15). "For what is highly esteemed among men is an abomination in the sight of God" (Luke 16:15).

It's possible to be wealthy but not worldly. Both the Bible and Christian history tell us about rich people who walked with God and brought blessing to others through their wealth. But I've noticed that the *leaders* in Scripture were careful to keep their hands clean when it came to money, and they didn't use their stature or authority to exploit others.

Listen to Abraham, who refused the spoils of Sodom: "I have raised my hand to the LORD, God Most High, the Possessor of heaven and earth, that I will take nothing, from a thread to a sandal strap, and that I will not take anything that is yours, lest you should say, 'I have made Abram rich'" (Gen. 14:22–23).

Listen to the prophet Samuel: "Witness against me before the LORD and before His anointed: Whose ox have I taken, or whose donkey have I taken, or whom have I cheated? Whom have I oppressed, or from whose hand have I received any bribe with which to blind my eyes?" (1 Sam. 12:3).

Listen to Paul as he addressed the Ephesian pastors: "I have coveted no one's silver or gold or apparel. Yes, you yourselves know that these hands have provided for my necessities, and for those who were with me. I have shown you in every way, by laboring like this, that you must support the weak. And remember the words of the Lord Jesus, that He said, 'It is more blessed to give than to receive'" (Acts 20:33–35).

"Not greedy for money" is one of the qualifications for ministry (see Titus 1:7). Therefore God's people have a right to know whether or not their ministers handle their finances honestly. I think this applies to anyone who lives by the free-will support of others, and this includes media ministers as well as missionaries, evangelists, and local church pastors. God's servants ought to receive adequate support, because "the laborer is worthy of his wages" (Luke 10:7); but they should use that support wisely and be ready to give an accurate account.

The covetous minister will become either a huckster or a hireling. The huckster peddles his gifts for money and uses his Bible and his congregation the way an actor uses a script and a theater audience. He always resigns when a better job comes along. The hireling works for wages and does what he's expected to do—but no more. The most important days of the week are payday and his day off. He resigns when an easier job comes along or when danger threatens the flock (see John 10:12–13).

"For the love of money is a root of all kinds of evil," Paul warned Timothy (1 Tim. 6:10), and he ordered him to pass the message along to the rich people in his congregation. James warned the church ushers to be careful in the way they seated the rich and the poor (see James 2:1–13), and he also called down judgment on the wealthy businessmen who exploited their poor laborers (see James 5:1–8). I get the impression that James was addressing professed Christians and not unconverted people.

Money is not neutral. Money is essentially evil, and we must beware of its seductive powers. Church leaders in particular must avoid the love of money: "Shepherd the flock of God which is among you, serving as overseers, not by compulsion but willingly, not for dishonest gain but eagerly" (1 Pet. 5:2).

The second myth we must bury is that money doesn't satisfy. How often in my salad days of ministry I declared, "Money will not bring you happiness! It will not satisfy you!" Alas, I was zealous and sincere, but dead wrong. Millions of people in this world are happy and satisfied because of what money can do. They aren't wealthy, but they're comfortable and enjoying life. The trouble is they aren't enjoying life at its best.

Some people don't know that the word *enjoy* is in the Bible, but Paul used it in 1 Timothy 6:17: "Command those who are rich in this present age not to be haughty, nor to trust in uncertain riches but in the living God, who gives us richly all things to enjoy." The theology here is clear. God made things, and things are good (see Gen. 1:31). God knows we need things (see Matt. 6:32), so He gives them to us and wants us to enjoy them. However, there's a caution here: we must enjoy God's gifts *humbly*, because they're gifts, and *carefully*, because wealth is uncertain and can be taken away in a moment. Most of all, we must not let God's gifts take the place of God.

"What Paul is warning against is not the desire to earn money to meet our needs and the needs of others," writes John Piper. "He is warning against the desire to *have* more and more money and the ego boost and material luxuries it can provide."[3] That's why Paul wrote, "But those who *desire to be rich* fall into temptation and a snare" (1 Tim. 6:9, italics mine).

The problem is not that money doesn't satisfy, *but that it does*. However, it satisfies only those people who are willing to live on a low level where money brings them their greatest happiness. That's what Jesus meant when He said, "Woe to you who are rich, / For you have received your consolation" (Luke 6:24). He made a similar statement about the overly pious and wealthy Pharisees: "Assuredly, I say to you, they have their reward" (Matt. 6:2).

H. H. Farmer wrote that "to Jesus the terrible thing about having wrong values in life and pursuing wrong things, is not that you are doomed to bitter disappointment, but that you are *not;* not that you do not achieve what you want, but that you *do*."[4]

The question each of us must answer is this: "What really satisfies me?" Are we content with having food, clothing, and shelter? Or do we desire something more than creature comforts? It's good to have the things that money can buy, provided we don't lose the things money can't buy. The people who "have their reward" have settled for second best.

Now we can better understand why the success gospel and the extravagant lifestyle of some TV preachers and their wives attracts the admiration and support of so many viewers: that's the level of life they desire, *and God may let them have it*. But that's all they will get; they've received their reward. And when life is over, they won't receive any more rewards. Their opportunities are finished.

The Bible exalts neither luxury nor poverty; it simply tells us to be satisfied with the basic needs of life. (Most of us in America have far more than our necessities, and we'll have a lot to answer for.) "Let your conduct be without covetousness; be content with such things as you have" (Heb. 13:5). "And having food and clothing, with these we shall be content" (1 Tim. 6:8). We must decide what our needs really are and live at that level. We can use whatever extra wealth God sends our way to help meet the needs of others. Simply because we have more income doesn't mean we're obligated to live more expensively, but it does mean we can share more extensively.

The third myth needing burial is that our responsibility ends with our giving. People who take that attitude often end up wasting what's left and letting the organizations they support waste what was given. Both are sins.

Everything we have comes from God and must be used the way He directs: "And you shall remember the LORD your God, for it is He who gives you power to get wealth" (Deut. 8:18). God is the Owner; we are the stewards. No matter what proportion of our income we give to Him, whatever is left is also under His authority. Giving 10 percent or even 50 percent doesn't purchase for us the privilege of wasting the rest.

Since we must one day give an account of our stewardship, we must be careful where we put God's wealth. A friend of mine who gave a large gift to an unworthy organization said to me, "Well, I'll still get my reward. I gave it to the Lord, and He knows my heart." Perhaps, but if she had really wanted to give it to the Lord and please Him, she would have investigated how that organization handled its funds and what was being accomplished. How honored would you feel if somebody gave a gift in your name to the Society for the Recovery of Used Bottle Caps or the Committee to Rescue Misplaced Earthworms? Biblical stewardship means that we give a worthy gift, in a worthy manner, to a worthy organization or person that will use it for a worthy ministry.

The theology of Christian giving is outlined in 2 Corinthians 8–9. Paul emphasized that Christian giving must be motivated by *grace* and not by guilt. The Greek word *charis* (grace) is used at least ten times in these chapters. Grace giving means giving in spite of our circumstances (8:1–2), giving with enthusiasm and joy (8:3–4), and giving in response to God's gifts to us (8:7). Grace giving flows from within, from a grateful heart; it isn't pumped out by force.

God's concerns are the believer's willingness (8:10–12), ability (8:13–14), and faith (8:15). When we give, God sees the proportion, not just the portion; and He sees the heart as well as the hand. He knows that we can't give what we don't have, but He wants us to be generous with what we do have. Grace giving requires an attitude of faith in the living God, the kind of faith the farmer has when he sows his seed (9:6–11).

But Paul not only had a word about giving; he also had a

word about receiving (8:16–9:5). An ad hoc committee, chosen by the Gentile churches, traveled with Paul to receive the love gift and carry it to the poor Jewish believers in Judea. Why didn't Paul carry the gift by himself? Why involve all those other men? For one thing, it was obviously too dangerous for one man to carry all that money. Also, Paul wanted the offering to promote Christian unity, so the various churches were represented in the mission.

But there was a third reason: "providing honorable things, not only in the sight of the Lord, but also in the sight of men" (2 Cor. 8:21). Paul didn't want to give anybody any reason for questioning his handling of the money. Hence, a representative committee. It wasn't enough for Paul to say to the churches, "The Lord knows what I'm doing with this money." He was open and honest in his financial dealings and wanted the churches to know what he was doing. His enemies would have loved to accuse him of dishonesty.

Paul's policy suggests to me that every religious organization should see to it that all income is handled honestly. This means that gifts are receipted and used for the purposes for which they were given. It also means that restricted funds remain restricted and that all funds are dispensed according to an approved budget. Sound fiscal policy demands regular reports to the board as well as an annual audit. The board must see to it that no member of the organization is profiting personally from the ministry and that the fiscal information is available to those who ask.

Like most Christians, my wife and I receive a lot of mail from organizations asking for support. This doesn't upset us because we appreciate knowing what's going on in the evangelical world. We've learned that the Lord doesn't expect us to support everybody, but He does want us to be informed. Some of this mail we immediately throw away because we don't trust the organizations that send it. What's left we read and consider. Over the years, the Lord has led us to give to certain ministries that we know are solid and dependable; and we don't feel at all guilty if we can't give to the rest. If God does want us to give, He guides us and makes the gift possible.

The ministry I'm presently with, Back to the Bible, helped to found the Evangelical Council for Financial Accountability (ECFA), an independent agency that polices its members to make sure they maintain high standards of fiscal and organizational integrity. We also belong to the Interdenominational Foreign Mission Association (IFMA), which also maintains a high standard for its members. The newest "watchdog" agency is the Ethics and Financial Integrity Commission of the National Religious Broadcasters (EFICOM).

Frankly, I'd be cautious about giving to any ministry that wasn't a member of a dependable watchdog agency. By *dependable* I mean an agency that has high standards and isn't afraid to discipline its members, come what may. It takes more than a list of standards to make discipline work; it also takes some courage, especially if you're disciplining a ministry that's popular.

While I'm issuing warnings, let me say a few words about those ministries that have a large number of the director's relatives on the board and/or on the payroll: examine them carefully.

And let me warn you about organizations that use questionable fund-raising techniques, such as inventing an annual crisis or two, or offering merchandise of greater value than the amount of the gift. Not everybody agrees with us, but my wife and I don't like to be deluged with mail—we've had as many as three donor letters in one week from the same organization—and we don't appreciate telephone solicitation. One week I threatened to get an unlisted number, not because the local merchants were bothering us for business, but because Christian ministries were begging us for support. Before they call, I have answered: NO!

I heard about a man who found a registered letter notice on his door when he returned home from a trip, so he hurried to the post office. After all, he might have won the *Reader's Digest* sweepstakes! But the letter—registered, mind you—was from a televangelist, asking for a gift to help his ministry through its latest crisis. The man knew he couldn't get off that ministry's mailing list, so he made two other decisions: never to read any more mail from that ministry and never to watch the program again.

A radio listener in Ohio phoned me to share a problem, and in the course of our conversation, he told me this story:

"I have an unlisted phone number. One evening, I had a call from ———— [he named a TV ministry], and they asked me for a big donation. I was really surprised, and I asked them how they got my phone number since it was unlisted. The girl just beat around the bush. 'Oh, there are lots of ways to get numbers,' she told me. Now, why would a so-called Christian ministry violate a man's privacy and then lie about it?"

"Unless we hear from you *today*, our ministry will be over at the end of the week!" Ever see that in a letter or hear it over radio or TV? I hope you don't believe it. How about this one: "If our ministry goes down, it will affect the work of the gospel around the world"? Who did "the work of the gospel" before he came on the scene? This kind of high-powered exaggeration just doesn't belong in Christian ministry.

Perhaps these are extreme cases, but they illustrate what I'm concerned about: unethical methods of fund raising. In the early church, God's servants paid their bills by working, by accepting support from individuals, or by receiving gifts from local churches. Paul wasn't at all embarrassed to tell people his needs and ask for their prayer help. No doubt some of his friends did more than pray; they sent him gifts to assist in his work. I see nothing wrong with writing letters to friends who want to hear about our work and giving them accurate information that can guide them in their praying and giving. Communication is one thing; manipulation is quite something else.

There's a definite connection between fiscal accountability and faithfulness in ministry. People who can't be trusted with God's wealth can't be trusted with God's truth. Our Lord said, "He who is faithful in what is least [money] is faithful also in much; and he who is unjust in what is least is unjust also in much. Therefore, if you have not been faithful in the unrighteous mammon, who will commit to your trust the true riches?" (Luke 16:10–11).

The greatest wealth in the world is "the kingdom of God and His righteousness" (Matt. 6:33). *That* is what we should put first. If we do, God will see to everything else.

I have a feeling that many Christian ministries, including local churches, will go through difficult trials in the months to come. God is shaking things "that the things which cannot be shaken may remain" (Heb. 12:27; but also read vv. 25–29). It will be a time of painful self-examination, but that never hurt any organization. It will also be a time of sacrifice and submission, perhaps even of persecution; but these tribulations should bring us closer to God.

"For the time has come for judgment to begin at the house of God" (1 Pet. 4:17).

11
RECOVERY

What then is the Kingdom of God?
It is Jesus Christ and, through the Church,
the uniting of all things in him.

HOWARD A. SNYDER

The integrity crisis won't be finally solved by the National Religious Broadcasters, the Federal Communications Commission, or any other religious or government authority. Such organizations may be able to help by providing some fences and guards, but the presence of fences and guards will never guarantee the absence of criminals. The crisis can be solved only by individual believers in local churches, *because that's where the media ministries, good and bad, find their support.* During my pastoral ministry, I was amazed at the number of fundamental Christians I met who were addicted to questionable religious TV programs; and nothing I said could change their minds. Thousands of people who should have known better supported and promoted PTL; and even today, some of them blindly refuse to face facts.

The final responsibility for changes in the religious media must rest with leaders and members of local churches; but—and here's the problem—many local churches won't be able to change anything *until they change themselves*. Religious TV succeeds because it has the support of church people who enjoy "show business" Christianity. The local church, I fear, has its own integrity crisis.

Whenever something false succeeds, it's usually a sign that something true has failed. A happily married husband and wife don't have to search for extramarital thrills; they're perfectly satisfied with each other. It has frequently been pointed out that heresies in the church often indicate a failure in the church: somewhere we got out of balance. I think this applies particularly to the present crisis.

What's been missing in our local churches? Why have good people felt compelled to seek for substitutes elsewhere?

Let's begin by noting a lack of *spiritual authority in our churches*. I mean by that, the absence of the lordship of Jesus Christ over His ministers and His congregations. Two days after A. W. Tozer died, *The Alliance Witness* published his penetrating article "The Waning Authority of Christ in the Churches," in which he affirmed that "Jesus Christ has today almost no authority at all among the groups that call themselves by His name." He blamed the situation on two causes: the influence of tradition and custom, and the "revival of intellectualism among the evangelicals."[1] I recommend the article to you and your church board.

Perhaps the main symptom of this authority erosion is the obsession of local churches with "independence." Churches and church members do what is right in their own eyes. The church member who doesn't like the pastor simply gathers together a group of fellow dissidents and starts a new church or else invades another church and tries to take over. Did anybody search the Scriptures to see what the Spirit might want to say to the churches? Did anybody call a prayer meeting? Did anybody ask under whose authority they were starting a new church? Did anybody ask other churches to pray and give counsel? No, it's easier to follow a leader with charisma and be independent.

If I understand 1 Corinthians 12, there are no "independent" churches. Churches may be autonomous and nondenominational, but not independent. "We are members of one another" (Eph. 4:25). Our local churches may have different forms of government and different liturgies, but we're all under the headship of the same Lord Jesus Christ. It may not look like it, but Christ is still "head over all things to the church" (Eph. 1:22).

This spirit of independence creates serious problems within our churches and among our churches. Paul warned us: "For I know this, that after my departure savage wolves will come in among you, not sparing the flock. Also from among yourselves men will rise up, speaking perverse things, to draw away the disciples after themselves" (Acts 20:29–30). If the sheep are under the authority of their Great Shepherd, they'll recognize false shepherds when they see them, and they'll not follow them (see John 10:4–5).

In the New Testament churches, leadership was based on commitment, character, and conduct. You had to meet definite biblical qualifications before the church would ordain you and submit to your leadership. In the church today, leadership is too often based on personal charisma: the "gifted" person, not the godly person, gets a following and builds a religious kingdom for himself. Too often, the important thing is personality, not spirituality.

Local churches often seem to have a difficult time working together and presenting a united, loving witness to the community. Many times pastors suspect one another and compete with one another, even though they preach the same gospel, pray to the same Lord, and claim to be obedient to the same Word. In almost every city of any size, there's usually one church that does its own thing and pays little attention to the other churches, except when some of their sheep stray to other flocks.

I don't know the final solution to this problem. There are days when I wish every community had a bishop to help keep the sheep flocking together and the shepherds working together. But if we had that kind of arrangement, I suppose some of the pastors would start competing to become bishop! One answer, of course, is a baptism of love and humility that would result in our obeying Philippians 2:1–18 and Romans 14–15. The answer is—revival. More about this later.

Another thing missing in local churches is *spiritual worship*. True biblical worship so satisfies our total personality that we don't have to shop around for man-made substitutes. William Temple made this clear in his masterful definition of *worship*:

> For worship is the submission of all our nature to God. It is the quickening of conscience by His holiness; the nourishment of mind with His truth; the purifying of imagination by His beauty; the opening of the heart to His love; the surrender of will to His purpose—and all of this gathered up in adoration, the most selfless emotion of which our nature is capable and therefore the chief remedy for that self-centeredness which is our original sin and the source of all actual sin.[2]

In the light of that definition, how do most religious TV programs measure up? *How do most local churches measure up?* "In the average church service," wrote A. W. Tozer, "the most

119

real thing is the shadowy unreality of everything."[3] Alas, how true!

Even with its shadowy unreality, the Sunday morning worship service is so predictable that we need not consult the bulletin to find out what's happening next, and it's so tedious that what happens next doesn't make any difference. Satan knows that real worship is exciting and that excited saints cause him trouble, so he works overtime to keep us from devoting all our God-given faculties to the adoration of the Lord. Read William Temple's definition of worship again, and ask yourself, "Are *all* these areas of my personality devoted to God when I worship? Do I even have the opportunity in our services to *totally* give myself to God?"

Some of our evangelists and theologians have so warned us about "feelings" that we've pushed our emotions right out of church and into the sports arena. About the only opportunity we have to express our emotions honestly is at a wedding, and even there we have to be careful. Evangelical churches are high on cerebration and low on celebration. Too often we go home after the sermon with a new outline in our head and the same cold feeling in our heart.

I'm not asking for fanaticism or emotionalism. I'm only pleading for the kind of worship that satisfies the total being of people who are made in the image of God. If God's children don't give themselves to Him in true worship, they'll either atrophy emotionally or express that feeling unlawfully. They'll continue to search for substitutes and gradually become satisfied with that which is not bread. We can criticize the media ministries as much as we please, but that won't bring the hungry sheep back to the fold.

A third deficiency parallels what we've just been discussing: *excitement and expansion in ministry*. How tragic when people must go outside the local church program to identify with ministry that excites them and challenges them! I realize that God calls some of His people to minister in parachurch organizations, in my case, Back to the Bible. But when a parachurch organization starts to take the place of the local church fellowship, something is wrong. When churches resist change and practice "business as usual," they are inviting members to look elsewhere for opportunities.

This brings us to the delicate subject of parachurch ministries.

Jerry White defines a *parachurch ministry* as "any spiritual ministry whose organization is not under the control or authority of a local congregation."[4] This would include media ministries. Many pastors don't approve of their members supporting any organizations that are outside the purview of the local church, even the good ministries. That was never my position, not even when I was ministering in a local church, and I've pastored three of them.

People who say that there were no parachurch ministries in the New Testament era are technically correct, but there were probably no Sunday schools or seminaries either. I don't know of any principles in the New Testament that prohibits individual believers and churches from working together to get God's work done. In fact, a parachurch ministry, in which many believers from many churches work together, may be closer to the kind of unity Jesus prayed for (see John 17:20–23) than are churches that are marked by dissension and division.

Paul's "charity committee," appointed by the Gentile churches, is probably the closest thing to a parachurch ministry that is mentioned in Acts. But keep in mind that Paul carried on a fairly independent ministry, even though he reported to the "home church" when he returned from a trip. He wasn't able to keep in touch with the sending church the way missionaries do today; in a real sense, Paul and his "team" were not unlike a parachurch ministry.

All my Christian life, I've been associated in one way or another with parachurch ministries, though basically I'm a pastor at heart. I was converted at a YFC rally, and some of my first Christian service as a teenager was with that ministry. When I resigned from my first church to join the staff of Youth for Christ International, one of my pastor friends said, "I'm sorry you're leaving the ministry." That bothered me. Was he suggesting that I was *sinning* by leaving the pastorate and working with a parachurch ministry?

During these nearly forty years of ministry, I've had numerous opportunities to watch parachurch organizations in action. I've served on the staff of two parachurch ministries (YFC and Back to the Bible), taught in a Bible institute and in a seminary, served on several boards, written for several publishers and publications, spoken at many parachurch meetings, and had the privilege of knowing many of their leaders personally. I think I can speak with both authority and sympathy when it comes to parachurch ministries and their relationship to local churches.

To begin with, I don't like the word *parachurch*. It means "alongside the church," and that is not an accurate description of any parachurch ministry with which I'm acquainted. Alongside *which* church? Which congregation in your community is the "true church"? If there *is* such a congregation, all the other churches in town are parachurch ministries! Does that make sense?

It's worth noting that in Great Britain, the word *parachurch* originally referred to "a congregation" that existed alongside the institutional church. It was an "alternative church," "the church of the future," and not a religious organization different from the church. Of course, that's not the meaning of *para-church* today.[5]

I wish we had a new word, because every time we use the old one, we're perpetuating confusion and division. Maybe *metachurch* is a possibility—"with the church." As far as I'm concerned, truly biblical parachurch ministries are working *with* the church and serving the church. They aren't doing their own thing "alongside the church" and competing with the church.

If that isn't true, I'm in trouble. During the week, I prepare Bible studies and produce eight or ten radio programs at Back to the Bible, a parachurch organization. Sometimes on weekends, my wife and I travel to a church where I'll preach two or three times. Am I more a part of God's church on weekends than on weekdays? When I attend a mission organization board meeting or lecture in a school, am I *deserting* the church or *serving* the church? In some mysterious way, am I moving "into the church" and then "alongside the church" as I seek to use my spiritual gifts? The more I think about it, the more ludicrous it becomes.

I have a pastor friend who feels that God can't bless ministries outside the local church. However, the last time I was in his study, I noticed two diplomas from parachurch schools, a large collection of books and magazines printed by parachurch publishers, mail from a parachurch agency that handles his radio program, and cassette tapes produced by a parachurch recording studio. Apparently it's difficult for him to be consistent about this matter. I get the impression that he sees parachurch ministries as a threat both to his own influence and to the church's budget. He's wrong on both counts.

If I were to capsulize some recent conversations, especially with pastors, it would sound like this:

"Well, PTL is a parachurch ministry," says my friend.

"There's no accountability! One good thing might come out of it: one less work asking for support! There are too many parachurch groups now."

"Do local churches ever have scandals?" I ask.

Reluctantly he replies, "Yes." He may have read 1 Corinthians.

"Are all local churches accountable to some authority outside their church? Do they all issue audits?"

Even more reluctantly: "No."

"Do you think there are too many local churches in your city?"

"Yes, I do. Every time you turn around, somebody's starting a new church. It's the last thing we need!"

"So the accusations you've made against parachurch ministries might also apply to local churches?"

"Yes, I guess so." Thus endeth the conversation.

Parachurch ministries usually get started in one of three ways. Sometimes the Spirit of God unites men and churches with a common burden and vision, and they formally begin a new organization to get the job done. Some of the early Bible societies and mission agencies got started that way.

A second way that parachurch ministries get started is that sometimes one man, or a group of men, will experience God's special blessing in a remarkable way, but the established church has no room for it. If the ministry remained within only one church, it might destroy both the church and the ministry. The new wine must be put into new wineskins if the blessing is to be preserved and shared. The parting is friendly, the churches accept the new ministry, and everybody works together. Organizations like Youth for Christ, Child Evangelism Fellowship, and Christian Businessman's Committee seem to fit this category.

A third way parachurch ministries get started is through the determined efforts of people who simply want to do their own thing whether anybody else likes it or not. A missionary is asked not to return to the field, so he starts his own board and goes back anyway. A florist gets converted and decides to start a new organization to witness especially to florists. (Instead of *florist* feel free to substitute truck driver, mortician, divorcée, Swede, or whatever.) Not all parachurch ministries begin this way, but unfortunately many do. That's why we have too many of them.

I've been told that this wouldn't happen if local churches would stop "restricting" and "suppressing" gifted Christians. After all, if a believer has a burden for some specific ministry but can't get the church to respond, why shouldn't he start his own organization? There was a time when I would have rooted more for the underdog, but not any more. The longer I live, the more funerals I see of ministries that claim God established them, but apparently nobody could keep them going.

"I feel burdened to begin a radio ministry," a man wrote me. "What suggestions do you have?"

My reply: "I suggest you start ministering in your local church right where you are. If God sees you're faithful and ought to touch more people, He'll open the doors for you. Please don't start a new radio ministry until God opens the door; we already have more than we need."

When Nehemiah and his friends rebuilt the walls of Jerusalem, some of the people worked right in front of their own houses (see 3:10, 23, 28–30). That's a good place for anybody to start. If all of us in our local churches would follow their example, we could start solving the integrity crisis. I'm grateful for national organizations that promote higher standards for media ministries; but as long as local church members keep supporting the hucksters and the hirelings, we haven't solved the problem.

It's taken years for us to get into this mess, and we won't get out of it right away.

Unless—and I write this in fear and trembling—unless God graciously sends us a revival.

12
REVIVAL

Will You not revive us again,
That Your people may rejoice in You?

PSALM 85:6

Do you have a favorite painting? I suppose a good psychiatrist could learn a great deal about us just by studying our favorite pictures. Maybe we shouldn't even tell what they are.

Well, I'll take my chance. One of my favorites is *The Prophet Jeremiah Contemplating the Destruction of Jerusalem,* which was painted by Rembrandt. When my wife and I visited the Rijksmuseum in Amsterdam, I bought a postcard reproduction of the painting, framed it, and put it in my study. I have it before me now.

I like this picture because Jeremiah is my favorite prophet and because his ministry encourages me to keep going even when it looks like I'm failing. Occasionally I look at the picture and say, "Well, old boy, you look defeated, but you sure were a success! Thanks for being faithful. Thanks for encouraging me today."

Jeremiah was a big man. Difficult times produce both giants and midgets. "When small men cast long shadows, it's a sign the sun is setting." Somewhere I read that Walter Savage Landor wrote that over a hundred years ago, and it's worth repeating: "When small men cast long shadows, it's a sign the sun is setting." I wonder how Jeremiah would measure us and our shadows today.

It's difficult and dangerous to be an individual, marching to a different drummer. Henrik Ibsen said, "The man whom God wills to slay in the struggle of life He first individualizes."[1] We might paraphrase it, "The Christian whom God wants to bless and use in the present crisis must have the courage to be different and the conviction to keep going in the right direction, come what may."

In the final analysis, we don't change things by reading books and agreeing with one another. We change things by making ourselves available to God and obeying Him so He can work through us.

What kind of people does the church need today?

The church needs people with discernment, people who know that the shame of one ministry doesn't demand the condemnation of all ministries. The enemy would like nothing better than for the saints to start discrediting one another and strangling God's work before a critical world. Satan, not God, is the author of confusion.

Read these excerpts from a few of the letters that came to my desk shortly after the PTL scandal broke. I'm sure they're typical of letters my fellow broadcasters received.

> My unsaved husband is more bitter than ever about support for any Christian organization. . . . This . . . scandal has hurt deeply the work of the Lord and it isn't easy be-

ing a Christian these days. It is touch and go in my household.

Please remove my name from your mailing list. You can thank Jim and Tammy Bakker.

In view of some very unfortunate current events, the congregation has directed our Missions Committee to secure financial statements from each of the organizations we help to support. [We were happy to comply. We have no secrets.]

What a disgrace is all this TV scandal! I just pray that more people's eyes will be opened to the truth.

I serve a God, praise His name, who does not tell me to send money to you. . . . He won't give His blessing to anyone of the PTL tribe—including you. May He have mercy on you!

I was surprised to discover that Back to the Bible was a part of "the PTL tribe." But that letter only proves my point: Christians today desperately need discernment. If we aren't careful, we'll play right into the enemy's hands, weaken the cause of Christ, and destroy the work of God. I can assure you that this kind of suspicion and overreaction will have tragic consequences for the work of God everywhere, including local churches and world outreach through missions.

As never before, God's people must fight the right enemy in the right spirit, without neglecting the work God has given us to do. Like Nehemiah's workers, we must both *battle* and *build,* with a sword in one hand and a tool in the other. Spiritual discernment comes to those who know His Word, obey it, and depend on the Spirit of God.

The church also needs people with devotion to Jesus Christ. I know, that sounds like a pious platitude; but how better can I say it? The question that Jesus asked Peter, He's asking us today: "Do you love Me more than these?" (John 21:15). The most important thing about God's people is not that we love lost souls or even love our fellow saints. The most important thing is that we love Jesus Christ. Only then are we fit to feed His lambs, tend His sheep, and battle the wolves.

"A revival is the church falling in love with Jesus Christ all over again," wrote Vance Havner. "We are in love with ourselves, in love with our particular crowd, in love with our fundamentalism, maybe, but not in love with Him."[2]

It shocks people when I tell them that I don't go to church to hear a sermon or have fellowship with God's people, although I enjoy both. I go to church on the Lord's Day to bear witness that Jesus Christ is alive and to worship Him. In fact, I start each day, early in the morning, by worshiping Him. If He has my heart, He can trust me with everything else He wants to give me.

I'm deathly afraid of personal spiritual deterioration, of having a name that I'm alive when I'm really dead. The fact that I'm involved in ministry is no protection. Even ministry can create opportunities for the enemy to work. The sobering words of George MacDonald arrest me: "A man may sink by such slow degrees that, long after he is a devil, he may go on being a good churchman or a good dissenter and thinking himself a good Christian."[3]

The present crisis won't be solved by Christians who get their food and weapons secondhand. It will be solved by people who walk with God, who feed on His Word, who have strength for the battle, and who know how to use the sword of the Spirit. We need a return to the old-fashioned spiritual disciplines of life that our fathers and mothers practiced, disciplines that our liberated generation likes to call "legalism."

We need to dig again the old wells and call them by the same old names (see Gen. 26:18).

The church needs people who are doers of the Word and not just hearers, because the crisis won't be solved by spectators and armchair generals. God pity us! We preach unity and continue to "do our own thing," even if doing it hurts the work of others. We preach separation from the world and practice compromise. We preach love and then secretly rejoice when a brother or sister falls. We're so tolerant of sin in our own lives and in the lives of others that we don't dare get too specific in our preaching.

We need revival.

Again, another pious platitude, but I can't help it. *We need revival*. New life. New cleansing. New love. New unity. New power. Oh, how we need it! How *I* need it! Not because billions of people in this doomed world need to hear the gospel. Not because the church needs a housecleaning. Not because we're embarrassed and ashamed and want to start looking good again. Not because we've lost integrity and the world doesn't trust us anymore.

We need revival because we haven't been honoring God and bringing Him the glory He deserves. When God is not glorified, everything else goes wrong. Revival deals with the causes, not the symptoms. Revival is radical: it goes to the roots.

Consider the words of Richard Owen Roberts, one of today's leading authorities on revival:

> There is absolutely no question in my mind that a revived people will glorify God in a way they cannot glorify Him in their backsliding. When men and women learn to glorify God, they can really begin to enjoy Him. Their

enjoyment will not be seasonal but eternal. When God is glorified and enjoyed, the main pursuit of temporary pleasures is abandoned with enthusiasm and thanksgiving. What was once an inconceivable drudgery and restriction of the free spirit of man will become pure freedom and pleasure. What was previously sheer enjoyment will become filthy and depraved conduct more appropriate to the vile denizens of hell than to noble citizens of earth created in the image of God.[4]

Let's get practical. What must you and I do to encourage the coming of the revival we so desperately need?

Repent. This means being honest about sins, both personal and organizational. It means despising our sins, confessing them, turning from them, making restitution for them, and taking steps to see that we don't repeat them.

Those of us who direct parachurch ministries need to make sure we've been honest with our constituents and loving toward leaders of other ministries. We need to confess a competitive and critical spirit, perhaps even a jealous spirit. We may need to call a summit meeting of Christian leaders, not for promotion but for prayer. We need to come with broken hearts instead of big heads, confessing our sins instead of bragging about our statistics. Our personal and organizational differences need to be confessed and new steps taken toward working together in love.

What I just said about parachurch leaders applies to pastors and church officers, missionaries, denominational leaders, all who are seeking to serve the Lord.

These words on paper seem so weak! God's Word says it so much better!

If My people who are called by My name will humble themselves, and pray and seek My face, and turn from their wicked ways, then I will hear from heaven, and will forgive their sin and heal their land (2 Chron. 7:14).

Return. Perhaps our ministries have slowly moved away from the purposes that brought them into existence. Then let's return to those original high and holy aims and get rid of everything that stands in the way of fulfilling them, no matter how costly the surgery might be. Let's trim our staffs and cut our budgets and work harder and longer to stretch our resources. Let's discover what Paul meant when he wrote, "As poor, yet making many rich" (2 Cor. 6:10).

Let's return to the fundamental principles of the Word of God, the familiar truths we talk about but don't always practice. In our preaching, our fund raising, our promotion, our management, let's be Christians first and executives second. Let's have more prayer meetings and fewer committee meetings, more time in the Word, more personal concern for one another. Let's find out what pleases the Lord, not what tickles the ears of the Christian public.

I'm sorry if all this sounds preachy, but keep in mind that I'm preaching to myself as well. Very soon some of us will have to step off center stage and make room for a new generation of Christian leaders, and *I want my last years of service to make a difference in His church.* I don't want to spend my remaining years routinely making radio programs, writing books and articles, and preaching sermons. I want to experience a fresh touch from God so that my ministry will help God's people everywhere get a new grip on their life and service in Christ.

Repent.

Return.

Rejoice. "Will You not revive us again, / That Your people may rejoice in You?" (Ps. 85:6).

For too long we've been rejoicing over the wrong things:

budgets, buildings, statistics, emotional experiences, popularity, academic recognition, influence . . . everything but God. *Our values have been confused.* That's why the religious movements of the past fifty years haven't resulted in revival. We thought that our crowds and converts were proof that God was restoring a sick church, but we were wrong. Our efforts didn't restore the patient; they only stirred her up a bit and gave her enough strength to turn over and go back to sleep.

I repeat: our values are confused. And we're so comfortable in this snare of our own making that we don't really want to get out! The vested interests in the evangelical world are enormous, and revival might cost us financially. To any pastor or parachurch leader who, like King Amaziah, is worried about losing money, let me say, "The LORD is able to give you much more than this" (2 Chron. 25:9).

Let's start praying for revival, and let's include the people we don't agree with. Bob Cook used to remind us in YFC that God blesses people we disagree with. Fervent prayer doesn't demand that we form a new organization or set up a mailing list. If all of us in our local churches and our various ministries would just start praying for revival, *and keep praying for revival,* God will begin to work. This is what Dr. D. Martyn Lloyd-Jones said:

> I shall see no hope until the individual members of the Church are praying for revival, perhaps meeting in one another's homes, meeting in groups amongst friends, meeting together in churches, meeting anywhere you like, and praying with urgency and concentration for a shedding forth of the power of God. . . . There is no hope until we do.[5]

Let's declare a moratorium on Christian competition. It's not really important who is the greatest preacher, singer, or author or who has the biggest Sunday school or missions budget. God knows, and God gives the rewards. Meanwhile, there's work to be done.

Let's love one another and prove it by speaking the truth in love (see Eph. 4:15). Before we go to press, let's go to prayer and be sure that we're obeying Philippians 2:3: "Let nothing be done through selfish ambition or conceit, but in lowliness of mind let each esteem others better than himself."

Let's have a sincere concern for the ministry of others so we can encourage one another and pray for one another. Many Christian leaders are hurting and need our help. Who is the pastor's pastor? Who encourages the media minister, the author, the singer, the missionary executive?

Let's not forget that Jesus left us here to be His witnesses to tell people how to be saved. Jesus isn't building a Mutual Admiration Society; He's building His church.

This book has dealt with an integrity crisis that you and I must help to solve. The news about the crisis may change, but that doesn't mean that the situation is better or that the problem has been solved. If the problem isn't solved, the church's witness will be affected for years to come. It *must* be solved.

I've been told that the Chinese character for *crisis* is a combination of characters that mean "danger" and "opportunity." This is a perfect description of the church's situation today, *but our greatest danger is that we may waste our opportunity*. If religious media people go on as though nothing has happened, the dangers will grow and possibly destroy the opportunities.

We have a tough assignment: we're rebuilding in a day of

reproach. By God's grace, it can become a day of revival; and you and I can help to make the difference.

"Whatever He says to you, do it" (John 2:5).

NOTES

Preface

1. Ralph Waldo Emerson, *Self-Reliance* (New York: Peter Pauper Press, 1967), p. 22.

Chapter 1

The epigraph is from the *Dictionary of Quotable Definitions,* ed. Eugene E. Brussell (Englewood Cliffs, N.J.: Prentice-Hall, 1970), p. 509.

Chapter 2

The epigraph is from John Bartlett's *Familiar Quotations,* ed. Emily Morison Beck, 15th ed. (Boston: Little Brown, 1980), p. 592.

1. Peter T. Forsythe, *Positive Preaching and the Modern Mind* (London: Independent Press, 1953), p. 28.

Chapter 3

The epigraph is from *The New Book of Christian Quotations,* comp. Tony Castle (New York: Crossroad, 1984), p. 226.

1. Joseph Parker, *The People's Bible,* vol. 15 (London: Hodder and Stoughton, 1900), p. 282.

2. Dennis J. Hester, *The Vance Havner Quote Book* (Grand Rapids: Baker Book House, 1986), p. 63.

3. Eugene Peterson, *Run With the Horses* (Downer's Grove, Ill.: Inter-Varsity Press, 1983), p. 88. This is one of the finest studies I have seen of Jeremiah's ministry and message as it applies to our present-day situation.

4. Ibid., p. 62.

5. Parker, op. cit., p. 289.

6. Jerry Falwell, *25 of the Greatest Sermons Ever Preached* (Grand Rapids: Baker Book House, 1983), p. 18.

Chapter 4

The epigraph is from A. W. Tozer's *The Knowledge of the Holy* (New York: Harper and Row, 1961), p. 12.

1. Jon Johnston, *Will Evangelicalism Survive Its Own Popularity?* (Grand Rapids: Zondervan, 1980), pp. 2, 13.

2. Andrew A. Bonar, *Robert Murray McCheyne, Memoir and Remains* (London: Banner of Truth Trust, 1966), p. 282.

3. Hester, op. cit., p. 186.

Chapter 5

The epigraph is from *Oswald Chambers, The Best From All His Books,* comp. Harry Verploegh (Nashville: Oliver-Nelson, 1987), p. 141.

1. Charles Colson, *Kingdoms in Conflict* (Grand Rapids: William Morrow/Zondervan, 1987), pp. 244-45. Used by permission.

2. A. W. Tozer, *The Root of the Righteous* (Harrisburg, Pa.: Christian Publications, 1955), pp. 52–53.

3. Tozer, *Knowledge of the Holy,* p. 11.

4. Henry David Thoreau, *Walden* (Princeton: Princeton University Press, 1971), p. 74.

5. Brussell, op. cit., p. 53.

Chapter 6

The epigraph is from John R. W. Stott's *Between Two Worlds* (Grand Rapids: Eerdmans, 1982), p. 15.

1. Castle, op. cit., p. 45.

2. Ibid., p. 193.

Chapter 7

The epigraph is from A. W. Tozer's *The Root of the Righteous,* p. 19. (This source has been cited earlier.)

1. Niccolo Machiavelli, *The Prince* (New York: Bantam, 1966), p. 63.

2. Rupert Hughes, "When Will Rogers Wept," in *Folks Say of Will Rogers,* comp. William H. Payne and Jake Lyons (New York: G. P. Putnam's Sons, 1936), pp. 152–53.

3. Alexander Whyte, *Bible Characters, Ahithophel to Nehemiah* (London: Oliphant, Anderson and Ferrier, n.d.), p. 236.

4. John Henry Jowett, *The Preacher, His Life and Work* (New York: Harper, 1912), p. 44.

5. Charles H. Spurgeon, August 20, in *Morning and Evening,* reprint ed. (Grand Rapids: Zondervan, 1980).

6. Hester, op. cit., p. 209.

7. Bartlett, op. cit., p. 742.

Chapter 8

The epigraph is from Oswald Chambers' *My Utmost for His Highest* (New York: Dodd, Mead & Co., 1965), p. 328.

1. Bonar, op. cit., p. 93.

2. Castle, op. cit., p. 191.

3. Ibid., p. 192.

Chapter 9

The epigraph is from Jacques Ellul's *The Humiliation of the Word* (Grand Rapids: Eerdmans, 1985), p. 120.

1. Quoted in Malcolm Muggeridge's *Christ and the Media* (Grand Rapids: Eerdmans, 1977), p. 127. An experienced media man, Muggeridge is very negative toward television and even got rid of his TV set. These three lectures, and the reports of the discussions that followed, should be read carefully by anyone in religious media.

2. The ideas here are digested from Ellul, op. cit., pp. 97–98. *The Humiliation of the Word* is a basic text on the relationship between words and images. You don't have to agree with Ellul to benefit from his insights.

3. Ellul, ibid., p. 42.

4. Ibid., p. 141.

5. Neil Postman, *Amusing Ourselves to Death* (New York: Viking, 1985), p. 87. This is a penetrating study of the influence of television on several areas of American culture. For an excellent study of the British television scene, see John Fiske and John Hartley, *Reading Television* (London: Methuen, 1978).

6. Muggeridge, op. cit., p. 81.

7. Postman, op. cit., p. 143.

8. Russ Reid, "The Bakker Affair—What Can It Teach Us?" in issue no. 135, October 1987, of the *reid report* (Russ Reid Company, 2 North Lake Ave., Pasadena, CA 91101). Used by permission.

9. Postman, op. cit., p. 123.

10. Peterson, op. cit., p. 12.

11. C. S. Lewis, ed., *George MacDonald, An Anthology* (New York: Macmillan, 1947), p. 102.

12. Mike Yaconelli, "Evangelical Gigolo," in the June–July 1980 issue of *The Wittenberg Door* (1224 Greenfield Dr., El Cajon, CA 92021).

Chapter 10

The epigraph comes from Cicero's *De officiis* 2.11. I found it in *Dictionary of Quotations,* comp. Bergen Evans (New York: Delacorte Press, 1968), p. 461.

1. Richard Foster, *Money, Sex & Power* (San Francisco: Harper and Row, 1985), p. 29.

2. Ibid., p. 28.

3. John Piper, *Desiring God: Meditations of a Christian Hedonist* (Portland, Oreg.: Multnomah Press, 1986), p. 155. I highly recommend this book as a discussion of a neglected theme, presented in a practical way, undergirded with solid theological truth. Piper's approach avoids legalism and antinomianism and impractical mysticism.

4. H. H. Farmer, *Things Not Seen* (London: Nisbet and Co., 1938), p. 96. I wish that Farmer were better known today. In some areas, he seems to have anticipated C. S. Lewis.

Chapter 11

The epigraph is from Howard A. Snyder's *The Community of the King* (Downers Grove, Ill.: Inter-Varsity Press, 1978), p. 16.

1. "The Waning Authority of Christ in the Churches" by A. W. Tozer was published originally in *The Alliance Witness,* May 15, 1963. It is also found in his book *God Tells the Man Who Cares* (Harrisburg, Pa.: Christian Publications, 1970), pp. 163–72; and *The Best of A. W. Tozer,* ed. Warren W. Wiersbe (Grand Rapids: Baker Book House, 1978), pp. 87–94.

2. William Temple, *Readings In St. John's Gospel,* 1st ser. (London: Macmillan, 1939), p. 68. For further discussion of the importance of worship, see my *Real Worship: It Will Transform Your Life* (Nashville: Oliver-Nelson, 1986). The serious student will find the bibliography helpful.

3. A. W. Tozer, *The Divine Conquest* (Harrisburg, Pa.: Christian Publications, n.d.), p. 90.

4. Jerry White, *The Church & The Parachurch: An Uneasy Marriage* (Portland, Oreg.: Multnomah Press, 1983), p. 19. White's approach is fair, and his conclusions are balanced.

5. See *para* in the *Supplement* volume of *The Oxford English Dictionary*, compact ed. (Oxford: Clarendon Press, 1987), p. 717.

Chapter 12

1. Rhoda T. Tripp, comp., *The International Thesaurus of Quotations* (New York: Crowell, 1970), p. 310.

2. Hester, op. cit., p. 192.

3. Lewis, op. cit., p. 97.

4. Richard Owen Roberts, *Revival* (Wheaton, Ill.: Tyndale, 1982), pp. 10–11. This book is one of the finest on the subject of revival, and the bibliography is exceptional. I wish every pastor would read it and take it to heart.

5. D. Martyn Lloyd-Jones, *Revival* (Westchester, Ill.: Crossway, 1987), p. 20. Dr. Lloyd-Jones's deep concern for revival in the church is evident in these twenty-four messages that are solidly based on Scripture. This volume is a perfect companion to the one by Richard Owen Roberts noted above.